O9-BUD-994

DISCARD

# DATE DUE

| | |
|---|---|
| | |
| | |
| | |
| | |
| | |
| | |
| | |
| | |
| | |
| | |
| | |
| | |
| | |
| | |
| | |
| | |
| | |
| | |
| | |

BRODART, CO.                    Cat. No. 23-221-003

ALSO BY MICHELLE SINGLETARY

*Spend Well, Live Rich*

**YOUR MONEY**
**AND**
**YOUR MAN**

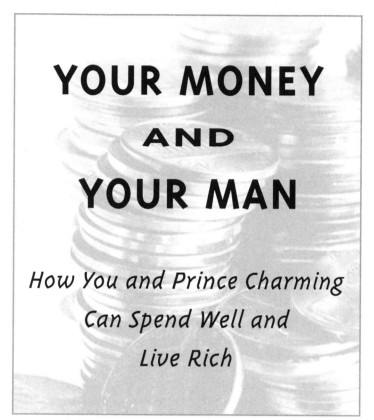

# YOUR MONEY
## AND
# YOUR MAN

*How You and Prince Charming*
*Can Spend Well and*
*Live Rich*

## MICHELLE SINGLETARY

RANDOM HOUSE

NEW YORK

*Your Money and Your Man* is a commonsense guide to personal finance. In practical-advice books, as in life, there are no guarantees, and readers are cautioned to rely on their own judgment about their individual circumstances and to act accordingly.

Copyright © 2006 by Michelle Singletary

All rights reserved.

Published in the United States by Random House, an imprint of The Random House Publishing Group, a division of Random House, Inc., New York.

RANDOM HOUSE and colophon are registered trademarks of Random House, Inc.

Grateful acknowledgment is made to the following for permission to reprint previously published material:

TEXAS SOCIETY OF CERTIFIED PUBLIC ACCOUNTANTS: "Financial Compatibility Quiz." Reprinted with the permission of the Texas Society of Certified Public Accountants.

THE WASHINGTON POST WRITERS GROUP: Material from the following "Color of Money" columns: November 16, 1997; February 22, 1998; March 8 and 22, 1998; January 17, 1999; February 28, 1999; February 13, 2000; July 23, 2000; July 29, 2001; October 25, 2001; April 25, 2002; September 22, 2002; May 15, 2003; July 27 and 31, 2003; November 21, 2004; and December 2, 2004. Reprinted by permission of The Washington Post Writers Group.

WASHINGTONPOST.NEWSWEEK INTERACTIVE: Excerpts from washingtonpost.com Live Online Discussions featuring Michelle Singletary, copyright © Washingtonpost.Newsweek Interactive. Reprinted by permission of Washingtonpost.Newsweek Interactive.

FAIR ISAAC CORPORATION: Information relating to credit scoring from www.myFICO.com, copyright © Fair Isaac Corporation. Reprinted by permission.

Library of Congress Cataloging-in-Publication Data

Singletary, Michelle.
Your money and your man: how you and Prince Charming can spend well and live rich / Michelle Singletary.
p. cm.
Includes bibliographical references.
ISBN 1-4000-6378-7
1. Women—Finance, Personal. 2. Man-woman relationships—Economic aspects. 3. Marriage—Economic aspects. 4. Wives—Finance, Personal. 5. Married people—Finance, Personal. I. Title.
HG179.S5145 2006
332.024'01'08655—dc22          2005050754

Printed in the United States of America on acid-free paper

www.atrandom.com

246897531

First Edition

Book design by JoAnne Metsch

ACC Library Services
Austin, Texas

*To Kevin.*
*Thank you for being*
*the mountain I can lean on.*

# Contents

# Introduction

In all the years I've been a personal finance columnist for *The Washington Post*, I've received scores of letters and e-mails from couples (many during the regular online discussions I host). I've had the chance to see how many couples mismanage their money.

It's heartbreaking.

Again and again, I see what happens when couples fail to communicate or compromise, marry people who don't share their financial goals, or act like they're roommates, not people partnered for life.

I've heard from couples with good incomes who are near bankruptcy because they can't budget. I've heard from couples who make major purchases without consulting their spouse. I've heard from couples who hide purchases. I've heard from couples who try to outspend each other like children fussing about who got a bigger piece of pie.

I've heard from women who boast about having secret bank accounts because they don't fully trust the men *they chose* to marry.

I've heard from couples who argue over who should pay what percentage of the household bills. I've heard from couples full of resentment because one person makes more than the other.

I want to smack them.

Here's a universal truth about your money and your man: Money may not buy love, but fighting about it will bankrupt your relationship.

How is it that people can proclaim to love one another, sleep with each other, and even have children together, yet won't do what it takes to stop fighting about money?

I know why.

And deep down, you know why, too.

Couples fight about money because they have "issues."

Perhaps your husband was overindulged as a child. As an adult he feels entitled to the best this world has to offer, regardless of whether he earns enough to pay for it all. Or maybe your boyfriend grew up not having much of anything, and worries now about having enough money all the time. The result is, he's so frustratingly frugal that when he pinches a penny, he dents it.

The fights are not about the money. They are rarely about the money. For example, I received a letter from a reader who wrote: "I grew up very poor and never wanted to live a 'poor' life as an adult. I was able to get myself through college and get a decent paying job. I married quite young, at twenty-one. He was twenty. Twenty years later, we are getting divorced. And the number one reason was the issue of money."

Specifically, the woman wrote, the divorce was precipitated by her husband's unplanned purchase of a truck. "He just went out and bought it," she said. "I feel horrible to have my marriage dissolve over something like this, but I felt like he had a total lack of respect toward the family financial situation. We had $20,000 in credit card debt and no money in savings. On top of that, he pur-

With that rhyme in mind, I've written *Your Money and Your Man* in four parts. The first part, "First Comes Love," addresses the financial issues that often drag dating couples down. One of the most important lessons from the first part is to watch carefully how your man handles his finances. His money management is the best barometer of what's in store for your relationship in the long term. If he jokes about not balancing his bank account or that his credit cards are always maxed out, most likely your man is not going to keep his money right. Trust me, Prince Charming won't seem so enchanting when he's messing up the checkbook and the two of you are being hit with bounced-check fees every month.

In the first part, I'll also discuss the dangers of cosigning for your partner before marriage, prenuptial agreements, the financial pitfalls of shacking up (oh, sorry, I mean cohabitation), the dos and don'ts of sharing intimate details of your finances, and the financial conversations you should have after getting engaged.

In the second part of the book, "Then Comes Marriage," I'll discuss the foolishness of overspending for a wedding, as well as joint accounts, secret accounts, and household budgets. I'll also talk about getting out of debt.

The third part, "Then Comes Baby in the Baby Carriage," will give you tips on how to teach your children about money and pay for their education.

Finally, the fourth part, "How You and Prince Charming Can Spend Well and Live Rich," addresses saving, investing, retirement planning, and financial priorities—as well as what to do when living "happily ever after" means "separately."

Ultimately, what I hope is that you and your man will find a way to have a relationship that is financially balanced. That balance can happen if you follow these three simple Cs—communicate, compromise, and set common goals.

chased season tickets to a major sports event. I emotionally left the relationship at that point. My family is broken. My heart is broken."

You might think this couple's marriage was ruined by money problems. Sure, the letter writer's husband put his family deeper in debt by buying a truck they couldn't afford. But the breakup wasn't really about the money. It was about this couple's failure to work as a team. The husband wanted what he wanted when he wanted it. Damn anybody else.

It was the last line in this woman's letter that confirmed what I've always known about love and money. She wrote: "In my case it was a case of disrespect from my spouse."

It's a lack of communication and compromise that torpedoes relationships, not a lack of money. Many couples think that if they made more money, their financial issues would go away. They wouldn't. The problems would just become more expensive.

This book is aimed at women in two different situations. It's for women who need to start paying attention to the red flags that indicate they've got some serious money issues with their boyfriends or fiancés. It's also for married women who know that issues precipitated by money may be weakening their marriage or, even worse, destroying it.

Although there is little data showing that money conflicts lead directly to divorce, money is still one of the top reasons why couples fight. Surveys show that the biggest strain on a relationship is managing finances, followed by compatibility issues.

A well-known children's rhyme comes to mind when I think of couples and money:

> *First comes love,*
> *Then comes marriage,*
> *Then comes baby in the baby carriage.*

When it comes to your money and your man, you will not live rich if you don't find a way to communicate honestly about your financial differences. You will not live rich if you don't learn to compromise. And you will not live rich if you don't set common financial goals.

Follow the three Cs and you will be able to trust your man with your heart and your money.

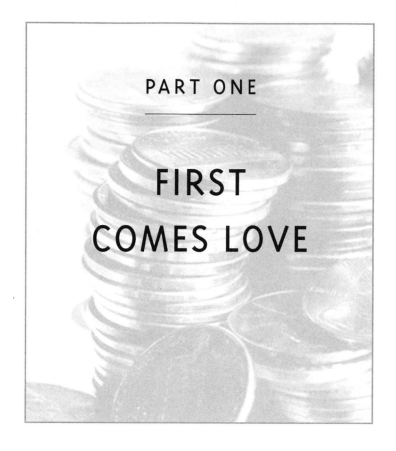

PART ONE

# FIRST
# COMES LOVE

# I

—

# A MAN IS NOT A PLAN

There are a lot of women who don't think they can become prosperous on their own. They think a man is a plan.

"As a single thirty-something female, I am growing increasingly disgusted with female friends who keep putting off financial planning—everything from contributing to a 401(k) to buying a house," one reader wrote to me. "They say, 'This will all be taken care of when I get married.' These are grown women with real jobs who seem to think the little black dress they use to potentially attract 'Mr. Right' is a better investment than real estate."

So should you wait to make major financial decisions until you get married? You'd better say no, because the reality is that Prince Charming may never come. Or when he does, he's likely to be supporting his first wife and their children. Or he may have two nickels to rub together, but one of them belongs to somebody else.

The fact is, an increasing number of women will end up managing money on their own because they've been divorced or widowed or have never married. Consider this:

- Although the gap between male and female life expectancy has been closing, women still outlive men on average (which closed from 5.4 years in 2002 to 5.3 years in 2003). The average age at which a married woman will be widowed is fifty-eight. (It's fifty-nine for women in a second marriage). A longer life expectancy for a woman means she has a longer time to accumulate wealth but also a longer retirement period to fund. While a woman who reaches her mid-sixties can expect to live approximately twenty more years, her salary, according to the U.S. Census Bureau, remains on average about three-quarters that of a man's.

- Women spend an average of eleven years out of the workforce caring for a relative or children. That time is usually spent not saving for retirement. Women, therefore, have to save what they can when they can while working in the event that they do end up leaving their job to take care of a child or an aging relative.

- Women spend as many years caring for their elderly parents as they do raising their children. Research by the National Alliance for Caregiving found that nearly three-fourths of all caregivers for people over the age of fifty are women. Forty-one percent of these women are caring for children at the same time they are caring for elderly adults. Further, even if women have brothers with whom they might share the work, daughters spend significantly more time and money providing care for elderly parents than sons do.

- For typical women of retirement age, Social Security accounts for more than half their income. The average Social Security check in 2004 was $955 a month. Could you live on that?

For African-American women, the news is even more disconcerting. Although African-American women have made significant economic progress in recent decades, many still lag behind in most key economic indicators compared with non–African-American women, according to a report commissioned by the National Council of Negro Women and the Fannie Mae Foundation. Some key findings of that research include:

- Half of African-American women say they are just getting by or struggling. Forty-one percent have household incomes of less than $30,000, compared with 33 percent of all women.

- Two out of three African-American women are solely responsible for their family's financial planning. African-American women are more likely to be solely responsible for their household finances in part because they are less likely to be married (54 percent of all women were married compared with 28 percent of African-American women).

- Only 41 percent of African-American women own their homes compared with 66 percent of all women. Most would like to own their own homes, but often don't know where to start.

- Forty-five percent of African-American women have children under age eighteen living in their household. Of those women, 42 percent are single mothers.

All these statistics show that women can't afford to wait for a man to plan their financial future. Don't wait to get married to buy your home. Don't worry that Mr. Right won't like your house. If he doesn't, you can sell and move.

It makes no financial sense to forgo the possibility of accumulating home equity waiting on the right man to come along. If you wait and never find a partner, you'll be a renter without a house, or a man.

## SINGLE AND FINANCIALLY SATISFIED

Only 30 percent of women describe themselves as "confident" or "a risk taker" when it comes to managing their finances, according to a survey of white, African-American, Asian-American, and Hispanic women age twenty-five and older commissioned by the American Institute of Certified Public Accountants.

This lack of confidence often results in women not investing at all or investing too conservatively.

Want to be financially satisfied whether you have a man or not? If so:

- Set financial goals for yourself. What do you want to do with the money you make—buy a home, car, take vacations every year? What will it take for you to live happily ever after financially? Will you be happy to work until you're sixty-five, seventy-five, or eighty? Do you want to send your children to college? How do you envision your retirement? Consider these goals not with a man in mind, but in terms of whether you can achieve them on your own.

- Get a sheet of paper and write down your goals. Then go about making those goals a reality. Don't just say you want to buy a home. Attend a first-time home buyer's seminar. Talk to someone at your bank about the many mortgage options available.

- Set short-term goals (establishing a three- to six-month emergency fund), intermediate goals (saving for a down payment on a home), and long-term goals (saving for retirement).

- Figure out just where your money is going, which will require doing a budget. (See chapter 16 for more information on how to budget.)

- Develop a financial contingency plan. Do some estate planning so that your loved ones will know how to handle your assets after you die. I know this is a tough topic to handle. Who wants to plan for her death? But you must, especially if you have children. At a minimum, you'll want enough savings to cover your funeral if you're single. If you have children, you'll want to leave at least enough to replace your earnings for a certain period of time, to cover the costs of hiring someone to fulfill your obligations at home, and to pay for your kids' college education. Many professionals with families seek life insurance protection equivalent to eight to fifteen times their annual earnings to support their families adequately. (See chapter 26 for more information on buying life insurance.)

- Get a will. And yes, you should have one even if you are single. If you die without a will, a state court will step in and determine how your assets will be allocated. If you're a single mom with minor children, the same court will decide with whom they will reside. And remember, if you're in a serious relationship—but not yet married—your significant other may have no rights to your property, unless your will directs otherwise.

- Get disability insurance. Many single women make the mistake of thinking life insurance is more important than disability insurance. Yet these women are more likely to become disabled. Keep in mind that life insurance is supposed to take care of your dependents should you die. If no one is depending on your income to survive, then you don't need life insurance. Disability insurance may be available through your job. If you already have an individual disability income insurance policy, update it annually to reflect any promotions or large increases in personal income.

- Make sure you're participating in your employer's retirement savings plan. Make a large enough contribution to take advantage of any matching funds your company may offer. If you don't, you're leaving free money on the table. If your employer doesn't provide a retirement plan such as a 401(k), then be sure to max out your contribution to an individual retirement account or other tax-qualified personal retirement instrument. It's also worth noting that changes to the tax code allow those over age fifty to save more in their 401(k)s and IRAs—what's referred to as "catch-up" retirement savings.

- Pay attention to small expenditures. For a month, write down everything you purchase, and determine those expenses you can live without. Invest the money for those nonessential items in mutual funds. At some fund companies, you can open a mutual fund account and contribute as little as $50 a month. Most important, you'll be establishing a regular pattern of saving and investing. And remember, you don't have to be a total miser; instead of eating out five times a month, try cutting back to two.

- Remember, cash is better than credit. Stick to having one credit card for emergencies and to build good credit. Otherwise, limit your purchases to cash. If you do use credit, pay the bill off every month. If you can't do that, you're in credit card trouble. In general, use credit cards only if you plan on paying off the entire balance every month.

It's wonderful if you do end up finding the right man to marry. But you don't have to put your financial life on hold waiting for that person to help you make important money decisions.

# 2

—

# A HOME IS
# WHERE YOUR WEALTH IS

Homeownership is without a doubt one of the primary ways people build net worth. Housing as an asset represents a significant share of a household's total wealth. The Federal Reserve's Survey of Consumer Finances found that more than 65 percent of the median household's net wealth is tied up in single-family residential housing.

Home equity, or homeownership, constitutes roughly one-fifth of total household net wealth, according to a 2004 study commissioned by the National Association of Realtors and conducted by the Joint Center for Housing Studies at Harvard University. As reported in this study, more than two-thirds of households owned a home, but only about half owned stocks or mutual funds containing stocks. And fully six in ten homeowners had more home equity than stock equity. Only households with incomes of more than $100,000 had more stock wealth than home equity wealth.

Home equity is especially important to lower-income households. Among homeowners with less than $20,000 in annual income, three-quarters have more home equity than stock equity.

Meanwhile, the median wealth of these low-income owners is eighty-one times greater than the median wealth of renters with comparable incomes.

Homeownership also gives you additional spending power. Home equity can give you the opportunity to access cash when you need it, for everything from buying a car to paying off credit card debt. In combination with today's historically low mortgage interest rates and double-digit gains in home prices, homeowners have set near records of cashing out through refinancing and home equity borrowing.

This doesn't mean you should use your home as a piggy bank to bail yourself out every time you overspend. But having a home with equity at least gives you options when you need money.

If you're single, buy a home as soon as you can afford one. You don't have to wait for Mr. Right to make this right financial move. And don't worry that your man won't like the house or neighborhood where you live. You can always sell your home and buy something both you and your spouse like.

So where do you start in the home-buying process? Here's where:

- Clean up your credit. If you need to borrow to buy your home—as most people do—then you will need to get a mortgage. That means a lender will be pulling your credit reports and your credit scores. Before this happens, take steps to clean up your credit profile. Start by getting copies of your credit reports. You can get a free copy of each of your three major credit reports every twelve months from each of the nationwide consumer credit reporting companies: Equifax, Experian, and TransUnion. Just go to www.annualcredit report.com. Once you have your credit reports, check to make sure all the information is correct and up-to-date. If you discover any inaccuracies, write to the credit bureaus to correct them. Later in the book, I explain how credit scoring works (see chapters 10 and 18).

- Determine how much house you can afford. The traditional rule of thumb is that you can buy a home that costs about two to three times your annual salary. But in many areas of the country, a heated housing market has rendered that rule useless. Still, don't let the fear of rising housing prices result in your getting more house than you can afford. Generally, a lender will want your monthly mortgage payment to total no more than about 28 percent of your monthly gross income (that's your monthly income before taxes and other paycheck deductions are taken out). However, it's not unheard of for people to be paying as much as 40 percent of their income for housing. It's a dangerous thing to commit 40 to 50 percent of your income to housing. To figure out how much home you can afford, visit www.hud.gov and search for "How much home can you afford."

- Don't worry if you can't put down the usual 20 percent. No longer do home buyers have to put down 20 percent. A variety of lenders offer mortgages that require a down payment as small as 3 to 5 percent of the purchase price. Heck, you can even get a mortgage these days with *no* money down. However, just a warning: If you put down less than 20 percent, you will likely end up having to pay for private mortgage insurance (PMI). This is insurance you must pay for, but it actually protects the lender if you default on your loan. PMI is paid monthly along with the principal and interest payments. Nationally, the average annual percentage you pay for PMI is around 0.5 percent of your loan balance. So, for example, if your home loan is for $250,000, your PMI will cost $1,250 annually. You have the right, under the Home-owner's Protection Act, to request cancellation of PMI when you pay down your mortgage to the point where it equals 80 percent of the original purchase price or if the appraised value of your home has met the 80 percent threshold. You also need a good payment history, meaning that you have not been thirty days late with your mortgage payment within a year of your request or sixty days late within two years. Also, you have to initiate the cancellation of PMI.

- It's still all about location, location, location. Even if you're single with no prospects of a husband and no children, still consider locating in areas with good schools. Why? Because when it comes time to sell, you will find that owning a home in a good school district can increase the value of your home.

- Get preapproved. Being preapproved by a qualified lender will save you the time and disappointment of looking at houses you can't afford. A preapproval letter will also put you in a better position to make a serious offer when you do find the right house. A preapproval letter from a lender is different from being "prequalified," which is just a cursory review of your finances that a real estate broker may make. Preapproval means a lender has actually looked at your income, debt, and credit history and determined how much you can afford to borrow.

- Check around for the best rates. I know this sounds simple, but some people are so anxious to buy a home that they fail to check around for the best mortgage deals. This is particularly true for folks who have poor or below-average credit scores. Even if you are credit-challenged, you can still negotiate with lenders. For example, if you have a below-average credit score (in the 625-to-650 range), you might offer to pay additional points. A point is a fee that equals 1 percent of the loan amount. If you borrow, say, $200,000, then one point would be equal to $2,000. Points are usually paid to the lender, mortgage broker, or both at the settlement. Paying one point will generally reduce your interest rate by approximately 0.25 percent. If you stay in the house for a long time—five to seven years or more—it's usually a better deal to pay points. The lower interest rate will save you more in the long run.

Be sure to check around for loan programs through the Federal Housing Administration and Department of Veterans Affairs or similar programs operated by cities or states. These programs usually require a smaller down payment.

The U.S. Department of Housing and Urban Development (HUD) website has a lot of good basic information about home buying. HUD has also created a very useful computer-based program designed to help potential homeowners. The homeownership Web video modules explain the basics of buying a home. These modules, which are available in both English and Spanish, include the following: "The ABCs of Homebuying," "Elevate Your Credit," "Easy to Understand Mortgage Programs," "Where to Find the Homeownership Money You Need," and "Ten Homeownership Facts That Will Save You Thousands." To find these modules, go to HUD's home page and type in "Homeownership for All."

Here are the various types of available loans:

• **Thirty-year fixed-rate mortgage:** With a fixed-rate mortgage, the interest rate is locked in for the life of your loan. The benefit of a fixed-rate loan is that your monthly mortgage expense is consistent, making budgeting a lot easier.

• **Fifteen-year fixed-rate mortgage:** This works the same as a thirty-year fixed rate—except, of course, you pay off your loan in fifteen years. With a fifteen-year mortgage, equity is built faster because early payments pay more principal.

• **Adjustable rate mortgage (ARM):** ARMs have become increasingly popular with home buyers because they offer a lower initial interest rate and payment than do fixed-rate loans. Adjustable loans are also worth considering if you plan to be in your home a short time. An ARM often enables you to qualify for a larger mortgage loan. With an ARM, your monthly mortgage payment may be fixed for a set number of years (three, five, or seven), and then be subject to change as often as once a year. Depending on the market, your interest rate could increase or decrease. The prospect of a varying interest rate can be scary, but many borrowers opt to take the risk to get their foot in the door of a home. Just be sure you fully understand the pros and cons. An ARM may make sense if you are confident that your income will increase over the years or if you expect to move in five or seven years—in which case you won't have to worry about the interest rate jumping when the ARM's initial term is over.

• **Interest-only loan:** Interest-only loans are just that—loans on which, at first, you pay only the interest on what you borrow. An interest-only payment option can come with a thirty-year fixed loan or an adjustable rate mortgage. The length of the interest-only portion of the loan can vary from three to ten years. After that, the loan converts to interest plus principal. The rates on interest-only loans can change as often as every month or be fixed for periods of three to ten years. In hot housing markets, people are doing whatever they can to get into a house. They fear that if they wait, homeownership will escape them. That's one of the reasons interest-only loans have become extremely popular. And this type of loan is an easy sell for some buyers, because they can qualify for a higher-priced home. Let's say that with a traditional mortgage product—where you pay both principal and interest—you would qualify for a $250,000 loan. With a thirty-year mortgage at 5.72 percent (the weekly average as of this writing, according to Bankrate.com), your monthly payment would be $1,454 (excluding taxes and mortgage insurance). But with a five-year interest-only loan at 4.68 percent, you could get a $350,000 mortgage with a monthly payment of $1,365.

• **Forty-year fixed-rate mortgage:** If you are in a high-cost housing market or rising interest rates make buying a home more difficult, you might consider a forty-year mortgage. Forty-year fixed-rate mortgages are essentially the same as thirty-year loans, but because the loan period is longer, borrowers can potentially qualify for larger mortgages. However, the extra ten years means paying more interest over the life of the loan. For example, if you have a $300,000 mortgage and the interest rate is fixed at 6 percent for thirty years, your monthly mortgage payment would be about $1,800, not including taxes and private mortgage insurance. Over the life of the thirty-year loan, you would pay about $348,000 in interest. The longer, forty-year loan would command a premium over the thirty-year rate. So getting a $300,000 home loan for forty years at a 6.25 percent interest rate would drop your monthly mortgage payment to about $1,700. However, your total interest payments would be more than $517,000. As you can see, the difference in interest is enormous, but the monthly payment savings isn't. There's also one other downside to this type of mortgage: The longer the loan, the more time it could take to build up equity.

# 3

—

# MAJOR MONEY MILESTONES

I hadn't even started my first full-time job out of college when my grandmother, Big Mama, began to tick off the money milestones she expected me to reach by the time I retired. Pay off your house before you retire, she lectured me. Make sure you save early in your working career.

How do you know if you're on the right financial path? When should you own your first home, begin saving for retirement, and buy life insurance? Make the right decisions early in your life and it can affect positively your family's finances (with or without a husband or significant other) for years to come.

With the wisdom I gained from my grandmother and information from the hundreds of experts I've interviewed over the years, what follows is a general guideline to the money milestones you and your man should be shooting for during your lifetimes.

## TWENTY TO TWENTY-NINE

- Make a habit of paying yourself before you pay any other expenses, including your mortgage or rent. Starting with your first paycheck, automatically set aside a specific amount for your savings (10 percent if you can). This is your emergency fund—your rainy-day money. And pulling out money for a vacation is not an emergency. This money is for the tough times, such as when you incur a job loss or a major car repair. If you don't have a cash cushion, when that rainy day comes you will end up increasing your debt load (in other words, using your credit cards). To avoid raiding the account, don't get an ATM card for it. You will need to have in your savings at least three to six months' worth of your monthly living expenses. This includes your rent or mortgage, grocery, cable, cell phone, and average credit card bills—basically all the money you have to pay out each month.

- Start saving for retirement. Figure out in your twenties how much you need to save for retirement. The median amount accumulated by those who have done the math is about $66,500, compared with $14,000 for those who have not done the calculation, according to the nonprofit organization Choose to Save. You can find a good retirement calculator at www.choosetosave.org.

- Buy your first home. Yes, that's right—even in your twenties you can become a homeowner. You might start with a condominium, town house, or small ranch house, but it's possible to own your own home before you're thirty. I did. I bought a condo at the age of twenty-two. I used a first-time home-buyer program that paid some of my closing costs and allowed me to make a small down payment. In addition, it's important to investigate first-time home buyer programs early on in your career when your income is likely to be lower, because most of these programs have income caps. Had I waited another year, I would not have qualified for my state's program.

> **"The habit of giving only enhances the desire to give."**
> **Walt Whitman**

- Build giving into your budget. On average, American taxpayers give about 2 percent of their gross income to charities. How much you give is a personal choice. But whatever percentage of your annual income you choose to give, begin your working career by making giving a part of your financial plan. If you tithe—meaning you give 10 percent of your income to your church, synagogue, or other religious organization— starting early will make it easier to continue this practice.

- Get a will and a living will. Many women, especially single women, neglect to draw up a will, believing they don't have much to leave anyone. But even a small amount of cash or possessions could benefit someone—a parent, a sibling, a niece or nephew. In a manner of speaking, we all have a will. It's just not one that we've written. In addition to a basic will, you should have a living will. This document, which may also be called a health care directive or advance directive, spells out what kind of medical treatment you want should you become too ill to speak for yourself. For example, it will state whether you want life-prolonging procedures. You will also need to get a medical power of attorney, which allows someone you name to make decisions about your medical care.

### THIRTY TO THIRTY-NINE

- If you're married by now and/or have children who depend on your income, get life insurance. If you're not sure how much you need, try the life insurance needs calculator created by the Life and Health Insurance Foundation for Education at www.life-line.org. Ideally, you want enough coverage so your beneficiaries could invest the death benefit and live off any interest earned.

- If you haven't written a will, do it, especially if you have children and have amassed a lot of assets. Consider a revocable living trust, a legal document that explicitly details how your money is to be spent upon your death. In simple terms, you create the trust and put into it important assets—such as your home—along with instructions about how these assets are to be distributed. With a living trust, you transfer all your significant assets to the trust and specify beneficiaries. While you are living, you benefit from the assets held in the trust. Upon your death, the beneficiaries receive the assets. The cost of having this type of trust prepared can run between $395 and $2,500 or more. The primary reason for establishing a living trust is to avoid probate, which can be time-consuming and costly. However, in recent years, many states have streamlined the probate process, reducing the cost and time it takes to settle an estate.

- If you haven't started saving for retirement, get busy. The longer you wait, the more you have to save.

- Start saving for college while your child is in diapers. On average, parents think they should start saving for college before their child is two, yet they don't actually start putting any money away until their child is almost six, according to a national study by Fidelity Investments. Think *compound interest*. Let's assume you start saving when your child is an infant. Given the cost of a public university education, an inflation rate of about 5 percent (for tuition, room, and board), and a growth rate of 8 percent on average over the years, you could fully fund your child's education for $250 a month.

## FORTY TO FORTY-NINE

- Even if you don't want to be bothered with the detailed planning involved in creating a living will or trust, you should still take the time to write a simple will, specifying who gets what. There are do-it-yourself versions—on paper and on computer software—but if you can afford it, it's best to have the will done by a lawyer. A lawyer can help you deal with tricky issues that may not be covered by the boilerplate do-it-yourself versions.

- If you haven't started saving for retirement, it's not too late. However, you will have to work longer than you planned.

- Buy a home. Homeownership remains the primary source of wealth for most Americans.

## FIFTY AND OLDER

- Update your will or trust.

- If you haven't bought a home, it's still not too late. A fifty-year-old woman wrote to me concerned that she had missed the opportunity to own her own home. "I'm just too old now," she said. Well, last time I checked there wasn't an age limit on homeownership! As long as you have the income to qualify for a mortgage, it's never too late to own your own home. In fact, it may be that you didn't have the financial wherewithal to buy earlier in your life. Now that you do, take the plunge. That's what I advised the woman who wrote to me. Six months later she wrote back: "I did it," she said. "Thank you for pushing me to make the best financial decision of my life."

- Save for retirement. Even if one day you realize that you're fifty and haven't saved anything for retirement, don't despair. It's still not too late. Actually, you aren't alone. The average 401(k) balance is about $51,000. Take advantage of catch-up provisions that allow people fifty and older to contribute extra money to retirement accounts.

- Pay off your home before you retire. Some experts are telling folks to always keep a home loan. If you're wealthy, that might make sense. But if your funds will be tight in retirement, getting rid of one of your biggest expenses could help you live easier.

- If no one is relying on your income, consider canceling your life insurance policy. Now take that money and add it to your retirement savings.

# 4

—

# DATING
# WITH DOLLAR SENSE

What's the first financial contact for dating women and men? Who should pay for the dates.

It's not the politically correct way to think, but do you secretly want your man to pay for everything?

The issue of who should pay—the man, the woman, or both—is still a big one for singles. A lot of women have expectations that the man should pay more often on their dates.

For example, here's a letter I received from one male reader: "I'm engaged to be married and my fiancée makes $52,000 a year and I make $20,000. She feels that I should pay half of everything. She also said that she shouldn't have to pay when we go out. I really lost a lot of love for her because of her views."

This guy has every right to be offended at his fiancée's views, especially since she earns more than he does. Why should he pay for all the dates?

In a nationwide survey of adults conducted for *Men's Health* magazine, the majority admitted believing that men should pay most of the cost to romance women. And the survey found that men are doing just that—picking up the majority of the tab for dinners, romantic getaways, and tickets to the movies or concerts.

One reader who found his reentry into the dating market financially frustrating wrote: "I try to date women who are professional with incomes comparable to mine. Sometimes I ask them out. Sometimes they ask me out. It doesn't seem to matter who does the asking, though, most of the time I'm still expected to pay simply because I'm the male. I had forgotten how annoying and costly it is to be constantly stuck with the bill on a date."

In his ideal world, this man believed that no matter who does the asking out, the cost of the date should be divided equally. "Of course, that may be why I don't get a lot of dates," he added.

Is this man cheap? I don't think so. Dating is expensive, and it's not fair to ask men to carry most of the financial burden.

## LADIES, GIFTS ARE IMMATERIAL

As you move past the "who should pay" stage, the next financial conflict in dating comes with gift giving.

A friend of mine told me a story that reminded me of why I feel bad for men when holidays or birthdays come around. "Once I was dating this woman and casually joked about what I should get her for Valentine's Day," he said. "Now, mind you, this was only our third date. She mentioned, in a very serious way, that she wanted something called a 'tennis bracelet.' I thought, *No problem.*

"When I found out what it was and how much one can cost, I thought she had to be out of her mind," my friend continued. "There was no way I was going to spend that kind of money on someone I barely knew."

His mistake, of course, was not his unfamiliarity with tennis bracelets or what they cost. His mistake was his unfamiliarity with the female mind. We women make Valentine's Day and other holidays stressful for men.

I'm not against gift giving, and I enjoy what Valentine's Day is supposed to celebrate. But too many women put too much emphasis on what their boyfriends buy, assuming it demonstrates their love.

Love doesn't come in a vase with $70 long-stem roses. Plenty of cheating boyfriends send their girlfriend roses, buy them fancy chocolate, or splurge on diamond stud earrings for them.

Every year the International Mass Retail Association (IMRA) reports that men spend a lot more than women for Valentine's Day. Men buy fancier cards and spend more because women's expectations are higher.

"Men are much more likely to buy big-ticket items and to shop at specialty stores for Valentine's Day," said IMRA president Robert J. Verdisco. "Valentine's Day is kind of a do-or-die holiday for men, who shop mostly for the women in their lives."

Look at what he said: "a do-or-die holiday." How ridiculous. And yet, I'll confess, I used to be a "do-or-die" woman. I used to put a lot of pressure on my husband when we were dating to spend money on me for Valentine's Day.

He didn't dare buy me cheap roses from a street-corner vendor. He knew that would look like last-minute desperation. I wanted the whole "romantic" shebang: a dozen roses in a crystal vase, a big box of chocolates, and perhaps a nice piece of jewelry or a dinner at a nice restaurant—a place that didn't have crayons for children at the hostess stand.

When we were dating, it was also imperative that the flowers be delivered to my job so I could walk through the office and show them off. Nothing, I so outrageously thought, showed me his love more than to give me the pleasure of having other women see what my boyfriend got me for Valentine's Day. One year he failed to understand this important point and presented the flowers to me during dinner. I was not a happy camper.

"What good are they going to do me now?" I sneered. "Nobody's going to see them but me."

Oh, how I made the poor man suffer.

In its Valentine's Day advertising, Blue Nile, an online retailer of diamonds and fine jewelry, encourages men to stay out of the doghouse by buying their sweethearts what they really want. "Diamond stud earrings are a sure-fire gift idea: One size fits all, they match everything and inspire appreciation that can last a lifetime," its advertising said one year. "If you've been together for a while, they're serious but not too serious."

Seriously, are they kidding?

What a shame that women are allowing retailers to manipulate them into driving their boyfriends crazy with demands to show their love through gifts.

So how about you give your guy a sweet treat—give him a break from having to worry about buying expensive, overpriced candy, bath beads, perfume, stuffed animals, or diamond stud earrings. All those things don't show that he cares. You know if he cares by the way he treats you, not the treats he gives you.

Give your man a hug and tell him his love is all you need. Real love means not keeping score on what your sweetheart is spending on you.

# 5

—

# WHY DO FOOLS FALL IN LOVE?

Okay, so you've gotten past the first few financial issues with your man. Things are getting comfortable. You're not monogamous yet, but you're headed that way.

When my readers write to ask when in the dating process it's appropriate to discuss finances, I always say the first date is too soon and the honeymoon is too late. Part of dating is getting to know someone you might want to marry. If, however, you're still at the stage of dating just for fun and you're not really ready to settle down, then I advise keeping your personal financial business just that—personal.

Don't share income figures, bank account holdings, and other financial details with people you aren't in a serious relationship with. However, you should use the time with this person to just observe and talk in general about his views on money. Find out what you like and don't like about the way he handles his money.

Most important, figure out what your financial deal breakers are. For instance, I grew up with a grandfather who was a heavy smoker. I hated inhaling his smoke, and vowed never to date a man who smokes. That was a deal breaker for me.

So what's your financial deal breaker?

Your man could be Mr. Right in every other department, but if you loathe bargain shopping and penny-pinching, don't marry a man who can't imagine shopping anywhere but Wal-Mart.

It doesn't make sense to continue dating someone and fall in love with him if fundamentally you can't stand his money style.

And yet many women do just that. I couldn't believe this question I received from a reader. She wrote: "I am a fifty-four year old woman who is thinking of marrying a fifty-six year old man. I have considerable assets—house, cars, investments, 401(k). My fiancé took early retirement, lives retirement check to retirement check, owns a home and a car, but has no appreciable savings. If we do get married, I do intend to keep our finances separate, but are there instances where I could be compelled to use my money for his benefit, such as paying for his nursing home care?"

Clearly she doesn't respect how her fiancé has handled his money. And if she's that concerned about taking care of him if he's sick, I wonder whether she respects him at all. My advice—stay single.

After years of writing a personal finance column, I know that very few people can change their financial ways without a lot of hard work, and often therapy. If your boyfriend is a spendthrift, don't kid yourself that things will change once you get married. They won't, and it will be your money he's wasting.

Here's a list of issues that some of my female readers admitted came up while they were dating their boyfriends but that they failed to address (and now fight about):

- She balanced her checkbook faithfully. He trusted the bank statement.

- She thought they both should be involved in the family finances. He thought the man should handle all the money.

- She wanted to divide the bills fifty-fifty. He thought the person who earns more should pay a higher percentage of the joint expenses.

- She was a die-hard saver. He couldn't save a dime if it was glued to his pocket.

- She thought every major purchase should be discussed. He thought any money he earned should be spent the way he wanted.

- She thought living without a budget was financial suicide. He thought budgets were too restrictive.

- She was a professional with a degree and didn't care if her husband made less than she did. He didn't have a degree and felt like less of a man because he could never earn as much as she did.

- She eventually wanted to be a stay-at-home mother. He didn't want to make the sacrifices it takes to live on one income.

- She was generous to a fault, willing to put her finances in jeopardy to bail out a relative or friend. His personal money mantra was "Neither a lender nor borrower be."

- She hated debt. He inflated his lifestyle by using credit.

Here are some questions you should be asking yourself and your man:

$ Are you comfortable with someone who is a spendthrift?
$ Does stinginess bother you?

$ Does it matter if your man likes to buy brand names?

$ Does it matter if he shops secondhand?

$ Can the two of you talk comfortably about money?

$ Is your would-be husband too controlling with money?

$ Do you want to control the money?

$ Does he respect your opinions about money?

$ What are his views on debt? On investing?

$ Does he resent having to give money to needy family and friends?

$ Is he too generous with friends and family and always broke because he's giving away his rent money?

These questions aren't about making money central to your life. They're about putting front and center those money issues that can disrupt a household. Honestly addressing these issues will help you decide if the man you're dating is financially right for you.

# 6

—

# IT'S HOW HE HANDLES
# HIS MONEY, NOT HOW
# MUCH HE MAKES

Is your man financially fit?

If you think I mean *Does he earn a lot of money,* think again. That's not what I mean. As you consider someone as a possible husband, you should be checking out how he handles whatever money he makes. I know love is powerful, but you would be foolish to fall in love with someone who does not handle his money well. You've got to know how your potential partner handles his finances so you can decide if that's how you want things to go.

Remember that the first C in a successful relationship is to communicate. The problem is that too many women think it's impolite to talk money while dating. Or they have something to hide (such as large credit card bills or a poor credit history), so they just avoid the topic, foolishly thinking love will conquer all—including past-due debts.

Money is crucial to our survival. You can't walk into a bank and plop down a bag of love and pay your mortgage. Only fools fall in love and think love will conquer all. It doesn't.

When it came time to think about whom I might consider for

marriage, I didn't grade the men I dated based on their looks (although many were mighty fine). Income wasn't high on my list, either.

Instead I watched how they dealt with all things financial. How my future spouse handled his money was too important to ignore: I harbored a lot of issues about financial security because of my upbringing.

I was raised by my grandmother, and she worried all the time about having enough money to pay the household bills. Part of the reason Big Mama worried so much was that my grandfather had a drinking problem and sometimes didn't bring all his paycheck home.

I knew that I couldn't live in a marriage where my husband didn't manage his drinking or his money well.

At one point I was comparing two guys I thought I might want to marry. One was the kind of guy to whom I only needed to hint that I wanted something and he would get it for me. My other suitor was, let's just say, less generous. He once said to me, "If I give you the moon, where do I go from there?"

You would have thought I had asked for the moon. I merely wanted a nice piece of jewelry that would at least put me on cloud nine (not the moon).

As I got closer to settling down, I decided to make a list of how each man handled himself financially.

Top on my list was whether he could fix things. While I'm sure there are plenty of women who are quite handy around the house, I can't fix anything. I remember once the toilet in my condominium overflowed. I frantically called one male friend, who worked in public relations. He told me to call a plumber, which I did. After picking myself up off the floor once the plumber quoted what it would cost just to inspect the problem, I called the other guy I was dating, a mechanical engineer.

He came right over and fixed my toilet. I realized that this was the man I wanted to marry. I know the value of a man who is handy around the house.

I'm joking, of course. (Well, just a little. Think of how much he would save me in repair bills over the years!)

Beyond his inability as a handyman, there were other things that bothered me about the public relations guy. He was too generous. It's nice to receive expensive gifts from a guy when you're dating, because it's *his* money.

On the other hand, the mechanical engineer didn't overindulge me (which I mistook at first for being cheap). When it became clear we would be seeing each other exclusively, he asked that we split the costs of our dates since we both made about the same amount of money and we both had savings goals.

Given the same two types of guys, who would you choose?

A. The romantic man who picks up the tab for just about every date and buys you just about whatever you ask him for?

*or*

B. The man who is cautious about overspending on gifts and is always thinking of inexpensive things you can do on your dates?

You might choose the A man. And it might work out. But I chose the B guy and I have no regrets. He is fine and frugal.

I decided not to take my relationship with the A guy further because I could see a future of being frustrated at his many purchases. How a person handles his money while he is single foreshadows your financial future as a couple.

When you get married, your financial priorities change, and you might not be so happy if your husband is spending the joint assets on things that don't improve your family's net worth. All the eating out, nice gifts, and expensive electronic toys may result in your delaying the purchase of your home or prevent you from saving for your children's college fund.

The dating process is the time to ask the right financial questions. Does your boyfriend have to have the best of everything even though he isn't making a big salary? Or maybe he is well paid but complains about having to tip the wait staff. Does he leave a decent tip?

When you go over to his apartment or house, are there bills piling up unopened? Does he buy a new car every few years for no good reason other than that he wants the latest model?

Really examine your boyfriend's lifestyle. How often does he eat out? When you eat out, does he order expensive bottles of wine? Does he take lunch to work? Is he always complaining about being broke even though you know he makes almost six figures as a computer operations manager?

Does his spending match his salary? Is he living beyond his means? Even if you don't know his exact salary, you can get a general idea by what he does for a living. Try the salary calculator on Monster.com if you're completely clueless.

Most important, ask yourself how the two of you will be able to afford the house you want when you get married given the way he spends. Once you factor in taxes and everyday living expenses, even a $100,000 salary may not go that far, especially in cities such as New York and Los Angeles.

If you realize and accept that you are marrying or living with a spendthrift, then you need a plan for how you will help him control his spending so that it doesn't ruin the two of you. Conversely, if your spouse is miserly, you'll need a plan or a therapist to deal with his excessive frugality.

And don't think that if you marry a man making a lot of money, you will live financially happily ever after.

I would think that in this day and age, I wouldn't have to tell women they should never marry for money. But I guess I do. Here's a real letter I received: "I don't love the guy, but he does make a good salary. Maybe I could learn to really love him. Is it OK to have money as a motivation for marriage?"

If money is a motivation for your marriage, you'll have a bankrupt life. Besides, financial battles are fought by couples at every economic level—low income, middle income, upper income, and obscenely rich.

A big salary is not always an indication that you will live a plush lifestyle. It's how he handles his money, not how much he makes, that can put you on the path to prosperity.

Choosing a mate based on how he handles his money is not the same as choosing a man based on how much he makes. You should be looking at whether your financial values match. And if they don't, you may need to kick him to the curb if you're not willing to do the hard work it will take to merge your different money styles.

Even if the man you're dating is your money opposite, you can learn to compromise (remember, that's the second C)—but the compromising should come before the commitment to be a couple. I'm not saying if your boyfriend has debt troubles you should dump him. But if you ignore the fact that you love to save and he loves to spend, you will be spending a lot of time fighting about money once you become serious.

# 7

## DATING AND DEBT SENSE

If you are dealing with heavy debt issues, you don't have to share them with your boyfriend. As one reader found out, not everybody can handle the truth. She wrote: "My boyfriend broke up with me regarding my spending habits. I was very hurt. Should you reveal your credit problems to someone who is just your boyfriend? There was no real talk of marriage."

Before a relationship turns serious, you should not share the intimate details of your finances. While it's possible that just through the course of dating your boyfriend will discover the state of your finances and spending habits, if you're not hearing wedding bells, don't sound the alarm about your fragile financial situation.

If, however, things are getting serious and you've started having the marriage talk—or if you are living with your boyfriend—you should be honest about your financial state of affairs.

Here's a letter I received from a woman that illustrates what *not* to do. She wrote: "My boyfriend and I have been living together for six months. He makes a good living, with no real debt. On the other hand, I have awful credit but a home with a lot of equity (owe $110,000 but house is worth $225,000). I pay the essentials on time but I still have about $6,000 in delinquent debt sitting out there festering on my credit report. My boyfriend wants to buy a new home. He doesn't know how bad my credit is. Should I tell him or wait until we decide to try to purchase the house? A large portion of the sale of my house would go to the down payment of the new house, so I would be contributing something besides a poor credit rating."

Think about one of the things this woman proposed—she is thinking about waiting until they are about to purchase a house to tell the truth. How do you think the meeting with the loan officer will go?

Not well, I assure you.

Despite the fact that she will be contributing a large amount to the down payment on the house, she's showing that she can't be trusted. And she may jeopardize their chances of getting the best loan rates. I've heard countless stories from mortgage lenders, brokers, and real estate agents of spouses or live-in boyfriends who found out during the loan process that their wives or girlfriends had racked up massive debt. Universally, the revelation caused a serious rift in the relationship.

## HELP HIM OUT, DON'T BAIL HIM OUT

If your boyfriend has some serious problems with his money, don't bail him out. Help him out by giving him the number of a good credit counseling agency. The same advice applies if you're the one in debt trouble. Handle your financial mess yourself.

And please, for goodness' sake, don't even think about paying anybody to "repair" your credit. All you're doing is taking money that could be used to pay a bill and giving it to some company that can't do anything for you that you can't do for yourself.

The best way to get control of your finances is to get professional help from a credit counseling agency. As you start your search for an agency, take care. Many credit counseling agencies—and I use the word *counseling* loosely—have been set up merely to collect fees from debtors in exchange for arranging a debt-repayment plan. They do little if any debt counseling, so many people end up right back in credit card trouble. (See chapter 18 for more on credit counseling.)

Once you're a couple and become more comfortable, it's natural to turn to your boyfriend for financial help. And he may turn to you. But merging your money issues can lead to more trouble than you think.

I'm always shocked at the number of dating couples who lend each other money, allow each other to use their credit cards, rent apartments together, and, in many cases, cosign on car loans. Do these people not watch Judge Judy? There seems to be an endless parade of women trying to collect money from deadbeat boyfriends.

Of course, many women have cosigned for their man with no problems at all, but do you want to be the example where it didn't work out? You should never cosign—for your boyfriend or anybody else, for that matter.

My grandmother, Big Mama, never cosigned for anybody, ever. I remember daring to ask my grandmother once to cosign a loan so I could buy a car when I graduated from college. It wasn't an expensive car, just a basic Ford Escort. It didn't even have air-conditioning.

"Child, have you lost your everlasting mind?" Big Mama asked in what turned into an hour-long lecture about the dangers of cosigning. "You ain't going to mess up my credit. You better go out there and catch the bus until the bank says you can get credit on your own."

And that's exactly what I did. I caught the bus until I could stand on my own two creditworthy feet.

If your boyfriend needs a car, buy him a bus pass until he can qualify for the loan. Think about it this way: If the bank, which has far more money than you do, won't take a risk on your boyfriend, why should you? And no, this is not a heartless way to think. You are just dating. He's just your boyfriend. Let him figure out how to stand on his own financially.

When you cosign, you're taking on a risk that a professional lender won't take. With cosigning, there are far more risks than there are rewards.

### *The rewards:*

- You could actually get a boost in your credit score. Because you both are responsible for the loan, your boyfriend's on-time payments are reported on your credit report as well as his. Paying bills on time is one of the top ways to maintain a good credit score.

- Your relationship might improve because you were willing to help out your boyfriend.

### *The risks:*

- You are on the hook for all of the debt. A lot of people believe that if they are listed as a "co-borrower," they aren't fully responsible for the loan. They think if the primary borrower doesn't pay, the bank will come after them as a last resort.

This is a wrong assumption. They will come after you for all of the money.

- Any late payments your boyfriend makes as the primary borrower will appear on your credit report.

- Cosigning could adversely affect your debt-to-income ratio, making it harder to qualify for future loans. For example, let's say you cosigned on a loan for your boyfriend for a $25,000 car. If later you need to get a car, the $25,000 loan will show up on your credit report as a debt obligation you owe. With too much long-term debt compared with your gross income, you may not qualify for your own car loan. Or if you qualify, you may not get a good rate because of your boyfriend's auto loan.

- In most states, if you cosign and your boyfriend misses a payment, the lender can immediately collect from you without first pursuing your boyfriend. In addition, the amount you owe may be increased—by late charges or by attorneys' fees—if the lender sues for collection. If the lender wins the case, your wages and property may be taken.

- Your relationship might not last, but the loan will. If, at some point, you break up with your man, don't expect the lender to be cooperative in removing you from the loan. Generally, a lender will not release a cosigner from a loan unless the primary borrower can qualify for the loan on his own. For example, let's say you purchased a home with your boyfriend, but a few years later you both decide to dissolve the relationship. You won't be able to walk away from that loan or have your name removed. You might be able to get out of this situation if your boyfriend refinances the mortgage. But again, that would require that he qualify for a new mortgage on his own.

Take the following test if you're thinking about cosigning a loan, opening a joint credit card account, or making your boyfriend an authorized user on any of your consumer credit accounts:

**Question: Would you be able to pay hundreds, if not thousands, of dollars for your boyfriend's purchases after you've broken up?**

**A.** I'm not worried, because it wouldn't come to that. My man loves me and wouldn't leave me.

**B.** My boyfriend has always been financially responsible, so I'm sure even if we broke up he would pay the loan or credit card debt as agreed. He wouldn't leave me with the debt.

**C.** I would have a problem. I barely have enough money to cover my own bills.

There's only one right answer.

If your answer was A, you'd better have a good amount of money stashed in a savings account. According to the Federal Trade Commission, studies of certain types of lenders show that for cosigned loans that go into default, as many as three out of four cosigners are asked to repay the loan. Do you really want to be put in that position? Can you afford to pay off someone else's loan?

If you answered B, you must be living in a parallel universe where all couples break up amicably and honor all the obligations they made to each other.

If your answer was C, welcome to the real world. You've got some common sense.

My grandmother Big Mama used to say, "A hard head makes for a soft behind." She meant that if you are determined to be stubborn, you will take a beating for not following common sense. So if you're hardheaded and still want to cosign for your boyfriend, at least consider these warnings from the Federal Trade Commission:

- Don't sign on unless you can afford the loan payments on your own. Keep in mind that if the primary borrower (your boyfriend) defaults on the loan, you could be sued for non-payment, or your credit rating could be damaged.

- Even if your boyfriend makes the payments on time all the time, just being a cosigner could keep you from getting other credit because creditors will consider the cosigned loan as one of your obligations.

- Ask the lender to calculate the amount of money you might owe. The lender isn't required to do this, but may if asked. You also may be able to negotiate the specific terms of your obligation. For example, you may want to limit your liability to the principal on the loan and not include late charges, court costs, or attorneys' fees. In this case, ask the lender to include a statement in the contract similar to: "The cosigner will be responsible only for the principal balance on this loan in the event of default."

- Ask the lender to agree, in writing, to notify you if the borrower misses a payment. That will give you time to deal with the problem or make back payments without having to repay the entire amount immediately.

- If you're cosigning for a purchase, do your best to get copies of all important papers, such as the loan contract, the Truth-in-Lending Disclosure Statement, and warranties. Even though you are a cosigner, you are not necessarily entitled to these documents. But if there is ever a dispute, you will need them—and you may have trouble getting them from the primary borrower.

## DON'T COSIGN YOUR GOOD CREDIT AWAY

I tell women all the time not to get a joint credit card with their boyfriends. Why?

Your credit could take some serious dings if your boyfriend misses payments, maxes out the joint credit card, or both. Just about anybody (like a college student with no job) can get a credit card these days. So if your boyfriend can't get one, that should be a huge red flag.

When two people sign up for a joint credit card, all activity is reported on both individuals' credit reports no matter who makes the charge. If your partner mishandles the credit card, it will negatively affect your individual credit score.

If you want to help your boyfriend get a credit card, tell him to get a secured credit card. With a secured card, he will have to deposit money into a savings account, and those funds will be used as collateral for his credit line.

For example, a credit card company might require you to deposit $300, and in return, you get a credit card with a $300 credit limit. The required savings deposit for a secured credit card typically ranges from $250 to $500. If you fail to pay the bill, the charges are deducted from the savings account. You can find some of the best secured card deals online at www.bankrate.com. Once you get a secured credit card, follow these tips:

- Use the card to make small purchases; the point is not to run up charges on the card but to show you can be trusted to make charges and pay them off. Never charge more than 50 percent of the available balance. When you are close to maxing out your credit card, it can lower your credit score because it appears that you're heavily in debt. If your secured credit card has a limit of $500, you shouldn't charge more than $250. And certainly don't go over the credit limit.

- When the bill comes, pay it on time. To show you can handle credit, pay off 80 percent of the balance.

- If he makes charges and pays off the card for several months, before you know it your boyfriend will be inundated with nonsecured credit card offers.

Not all secured credit cards are the same. In fact, there are many unscrupulous companies offering credit cards with high fees. And of course there are credit offers that are downright scams. Here's what you should watch for with secured cards:

- Avoid companies that offer a secured card with a laundry list of fees. Some come with an annual membership fee (as high as $150), a setup or application fee (as high as $70), a monthly maintenance fee (typically about $3.50), and/or an Internet access fee. You might even be charged an overlimit fee (typically about $30) if you access the full amount or most of your available credit.

- Avoid unusually high interest rates—although if you pay off your balance every month, you don't have to worry about a high rate.

- Some secured credit card insurers may even allow you to charge the amount that you are supposed to deposit in a savings account as security for the credit card. Don't do it. If you don't have the money to get a secured credit card, wait until you do. Companies that issue secured cards have introduced this hybrid type of card because often people with no credit or bad credit don't have the money for the security deposit. But it's a bad deal because you immediately incur high interest rate charges, typically in the double digits.

## PLAYING BANKER TO YOUR BOYFRIEND

> **"Boundless in your charity, but shrewd and cautious as a lender, you delight all those today whom you made beggars the day before."**
>
> **Franz Grillparzer**

So you're considering loaning your boyfriend some money. I understand how it may happen. He's down on his luck. He's lost his job. He's in graduate school. He's going through a divorce and is short on cash. He's a bad saver. You love him and want to help him out.

I don't believe that we should neither lenders nor borrowers be. Life happens. People get into financial trouble. Often getting a loan from a bank or credit union is not an option. So people turn to family, friends, co-workers—and often girlfriends.

If you can afford to either give or lend someone money who is in need, that's an admirable thing to do. However, you have to be smart about playing banker to your boyfriend. Take a look at what happened to these two women who submitted questions to me during an online discussion I was having about love and money.

One woman wrote: "I borrowed $10,000 from my retirement account at work to lend to my boyfriend (I know . . . very stupid thing to do). He faithfully paid me back for seven months and then stopped calling me. He lives out of state. When I finally got in touch with him, I had to beg him to send a payment. He sent $500. That's it. Needless to say, we are not together anymore and he still won't pay and gets an attitude with me when I bring up the subject. I would like to know what other recourse I have, if any?"

Another wrote: "I foolishly got a loan in my name for my now ex-boyfriend. He still owes me about $2,900 from a $3,500 loan. We were together for three years. We are not on good terms and I feel bad asking him for the money and just calling for that one reason."

In both cases I advised the women to take their ex-boyfriends to small claims court. But chances are they will never see that money again.

In the case of the woman who borrowed money from her retirement account, the situation could be even more costly. First, she will lose the potential return that the money could be earning. If she loses her job or can't pay back the loan, she will be hit with a 10 percent penalty by the IRS for early withdrawal from her retirement plan. In addition, she will have to pay ordinary income taxes on the money. Let's suppose she is in the 35 percent tax bracket. Roughly, she could end up owing the federal government about $4,500 in taxes and penalties.

It's fine if you want to lend your boyfriend money, but at the very least follow these guidelines to ensure you don't end up falling in love and breaking your bank:

- Never lend what you cannot afford to lose. If lending the money is going to put you in a financial bind, don't do it. Make sure any money you lend is money you can live without. When you lend money, think of it as a gift. That doesn't mean you don't want or shouldn't ask for it back, but if you *need* it back, you can't afford to lend it.

- Don't harbor ill feelings if you aren't paid back. I'm sure in many cases your ex (which I'm sure he will be if he stiffs you) is off enjoying his life and your money without giving you a second thought. If you need your money, don't stop trying to collect it. But at some point, you have to let go of the negative feelings.

- Don't beat yourself up for not spotting a deadbeat. Professional lenders have at their disposal sophisticated credit-scoring systems to help them determine who will pay them back—and still they get stiffed. We expect people to honor their word and debts. But when they don't, it doesn't necessarily mean you weren't a shrewd or cautious lender.

- Draw up a loan agreement. If your boyfriend intends to pay you back, he shouldn't be offended. If he balks, drive him to the nearest bank.

Of course, having a promissory note doesn't mean your boyfriend will keep his promise and pay you back, but it provides a strong piece of evidence in the event that you take him to small claims court. And you should definitely take his butt to small claims court if he fails to pay you back (and he should do the same if you stiff him).

## SAMPLE PERSONAL LOAN AGREEMENT

The lender(s) _____

The borrower(s) _____

Length of loan: (weeks/months/years): _____

Total loan amount: $_____

Annual percentage rate charged: _____%

Repayment conditions: The borrower(s) agrees to repay the loan amount on the _____ day of each month/week.

Late charge: Any payment not paid within five (5) days of the due date shall be subject to a late fee of $_____.

Total payment due at the end of this loan agreement: $_____.

Prepayment: The borrower(s) has the right to prepay the entire loan amount at any time. Interest will only be due for the time the loan is outstanding.

Co-borrowers: All borrowers listed in this agreement shall be equally responsible for paying the entire balance due on the loan; in other words, if one borrower decides not to pay, the co-borrower will still be responsible for the entire loan balance, including any interest and late charges due.

Default: If for any reason the borrower(s) fails to make _____ number of payments on time, the loan shall be in default. The lender(s) can then demand immediate payment of the entire remaining unpaid loan balance, including any interest and late fees.

Legal fees: If this loan results in legal action for nonpayment, then the borrower(s) agrees to pay any attorney or court fees or both associated with the collection of the unpaid loan balance.

As a legal adult 18 years or older, I am fully responsible for paying back the full amount of this loan.

Notarized signature of

Borrower: _____

Co-borrower: _____

Lender(s): _____

_____

Date of loan agreement: _____

Notary signature:

_____

Notary seal

Date: _____

# 8

—

# FIRST COMES LOVE,
# THEN COHABITATION

On the surface, it might seem to make sense for two people who are spending a lot of time together to give up paying rent and utilities for two apartments and set up one household. But while it's generally true that two can live cheaper than one, that's only if the two stay together. The cost of a breakup—a frequent occurrence—can be substantial. As for the children, there is much research that suggests they do not fare as well in alternative family structures as they do living with two married (well-adjusted) biological parents.

I don't believe couples should live together to try out a simulated marriage, or to save money—even when they are engaged to be married. My belief in this case is not based just on my values as a Christian but also on numerous studies and surveys, not to mention the personal experiences of many readers of my syndicated column for *The Washington Post*.

"Essentially, if it doesn't work out, it's like a divorce, except you don't have a legal leg to stand on," said Lisa, twenty-nine, a reader who wrote to me.

Lisa and her boyfriend lived together in an apartment in Virginia for three years before they decided to rent a house. Three months after moving into the house, the relationship soured and she moved out.

What had originally been a cost-saving move turned into a financial mess. I asked Lisa to tally up what the experience cost her. Here's a partial list of her expenses:

She had to pay $2,850 in rent on the house she was no longer sharing with her boyfriend. (If you cosign a lease, you are financially obligated for your share of the rent even if you vacate the property.)

In Lisa's case, she had to pay her boyfriend her share of the rent for the house she no longer occupied plus rent on her new apartment.

Lisa left behind about $4,000 worth of household goods. (She said it wasn't worth the aggravation; nor did she want to fight to try to reclaim the items.)

She spent $850 to buy some of the same household items—an iron, shower curtains, a television, and other personal products—for her new apartment.

She spent $100 on newspaper ads, trying to find someone to take over her half of the lease on the house she had rented with her ex. She also had to hope that her ex accepted the new roommate she found; otherwise she would have to continue to pay her share of the rent until the lease was up. (If the breakup was acrimonious—and many are—your ex may not be too amenable to accepting a new roommate.)

"I moved in with my boyfriend in the interest of saving money, but it was the most uncomfortable time of my life," Lisa said. "Funny thing was, we wanted the whole thing—the nice house, fireplace, and yard—just not marriage. But you think if it ends you can split up your stuff and work everything out like adults. Simple me."

She's right. She was simple to think not getting married was going to make the dissolution of their relationship financially easier. It doesn't.

It is not necessarily cheaper when cohabitating couples break up than when married couples divorce. That's because these days, cohabitating couples do everything married couples do—have children, merge bank accounts, open joint credit card accounts, and buy property together.

Here's another example of a breakup that went financially bad. A reader wrote: "In the early '90s, I lived in San Francisco with my fiancé and all the utilities were in my name only. When I broke up with him, I moved to Nevada, removing my name from the lease. However, I forgot to take the utilities out of my name. My ex continued to live in the apartment. At some point, he moved out. He let someone else move in and that person did not make the payments to the various utility companies. Several months ago I attempted to purchase a new car and was told my credit score was low because of unpaid utility bills. My credit is now suffering."

The woman wanted to know if her ex-fiancé could be held liable for the bills since he'd kept the utilities under her name.

Unfortunately, I had to tell this woman that she was stuck with those bills. Her ex can't be held liable for utility charges he didn't run up (and remember, it was she who forgot to take the utilities out of her name). As for her credit score, I had good news and bad news. The bad news was that since the bill was in her name, she was responsible for the debt. What was reported to the credit bureau was correct. However, she could sue the tenants who ran up the charges in small claims court. The good news was, after seven years the bad debt information has to be removed from her credit report. But until then, the best way for her to build her credit back up would be to pay her bills on time, all the time.

Since 1880, the Census Bureau has asked people to describe

their household relationships. In 1990, "unmarried partner" was added as a possible response to acknowledge the growing complexity of American households and the tendency for couples to live together before marriage.

The statistics show how times have changed. The number of married households has dropped from nearly 80 percent in the 1950s to about 50 percent in 2003, according to U.S. Census Bureau figures. In 2003, there were 4.6 million cohabiting couples. These couples constituted 4.2 percent of all households, up from 2.9 percent in 1996.

I know living together is the "in" thing to do, but unmarried couples face great difficulty establishing financial security for their partners and their families because many of the rules and regulations governing those areas are geared toward married couples.

There are more than 1,100 federal statutory provisions in which being married gives you certain benefits, rights, and privileges, according to a report by the Government Accountability Office. Here are some of the laws that favor marriage:

• **Social Security:** If your divorced spouse dies, you can receive benefits as a widow if the marriage lasted ten years or more. If you marry and get divorced after at least ten years of marriage, you can collect retirement benefits on your former spouse's Social Security record if you are at least age sixty-two and if your former spouse is entitled to or receiving benefits. You get no such benefit by living together.

• **Veterans' benefits:** Veterans' benefits include pensions, indemnity compensation for service-connected deaths, medical care, nursing home care, educational assistance, and housing. Husbands or wives of veterans have many rights and privileges by virtue of the marital relationship.

• **Taxation:** Marital status figures quite a bit in federal tax law. For example, under the tax code, a single taxpayer may exclude up to $250,000 of profit from the sale of her personal principal residence. Married couples filing jointly may exclude up to $500,000 on the sale of their home. (To be eligible for the exclusion, your home must have been owned by you and used as your main home for a period of at least two years out of the five years prior to its sale or exchange. The required two years of ownership does not have to be continuous.) In addition, for many people it's no longer true that there is a "marriage penalty" under which a couple earning about the same and filing jointly would have a greater tax liability than if they had filed as two single persons. An increase in the standard deduction for couples whose filing status is married filing jointly largely eliminated the marriage penalty.

• **Retirement accounts:** Under current law, when a retirement plan participant dies, plan benefits must be distributed in a lump sum or remain in the plan to be distributed in accordance with the minimum distribution requirements. This problem does not exist if the beneficiary is the deceased participant's surviving spouse, because the surviving spouse may transfer plan benefits to an IRA or a retirement plan in which she is a participant. This entitlement is valuable because (a) it allows the surviving spouse to defer taxation of the proceeds, often until the survivor is in a lower tax bracket; and (b) it protects the surviving spouse from being forced to withdraw from an investment plan when its value may be depressed.

• **Real estate:** There is a form of property ownership reserved only for husbands and wives. Under a tenancy-by-the-entirety arrangement, both husband and wife own an undivided interest in the property. Unless both parties owe money to a creditor, the house cannot be attached. On the death of one party, the entire property will be owned by the survivor, and no probate will be necessary. Thus, if you are married, and want to avoid probate, you should make sure that the title to your property is held in tenancy by the entirety. Here's another benefit: If one spouse has a debt or judgment against him or her, the bill collector may not attach any portion of the real estate. Only a bill collector who was owed by *both* the husband and the wife could make a claim on the real estate.

• **Estate and gift tax:** When your spouse dies, his estate can pass on to you without being taxed. This exemption is only available to married couples. There is usually no tax if you make a gift to your spouse.

• **Federal loans and guarantees:** Under many federal loan programs, marital status is a factor in determining the amount of federal assistance to which a person is entitled as well as the repayment schedule. This category includes education loan programs, housing loan programs for veterans, and provisions governing agricultural price supports and loan programs that are affected by the spousal relationship.

• **Employment benefits:** Marital status comes into play in many different ways in federal laws relating to employment in the private sector. This category includes laws that address the rights of employees under employer-sponsored employee benefit plans such as a 401(k) plan; continuation of employer-sponsored health benefits after events like the death or divorce of the employee; and the right of an employee to take unpaid leave in order to care for a seriously ill spouse.

The research is clear: Getting married and maintaining a healthy union in which both partners communicate well about money can be financially beneficial. According to the Alliance for Marriage, children whose parents are not married are five times more likely to be poor, four times more likely to engage in criminal behavior, and three times more likely to become welfare recipients when they reach adulthood.

That's not to say that if you don't get married, you will be poor. But marriage has a powerful wealth-accumulation effect. For example, one study found that over a comparable period of time, and holding constant for income level, married couples in their twenties and thirties with children tended to reach a median net worth of $26,000, while cohabiting couples reached a median net worth of just $1,000. More often, the married couples received financial assistance from in-laws, according to the study.

Married older couples also have higher median incomes and net worth than older adults who are widowed, divorced, or never married, according to a study published in the *Journal of Marriage and Family*. The authors of this study, Purdue University researchers Janet Wilmoth and Gregor Koso, concluded that the potential financial benefits of marriage include increased homeownership, insurance coverage for spouses, larger savings, and survivor pension benefits.

Certainly you can have financial security if you are single, a single parent, divorced, or widowed. But given the findings of the Purdue research, a good financial plan is especially important for those who have never been married or are separated, divorced, or widowed.

### BREAKING UP IS HARD TO DO—AND EXPENSIVE

After the dissolution of cohabiting unions, men's economic standing is only moderately affected, whereas women experience a significant decrease in their economic standing. A substantial portion end up in poverty, according to findings in the 2005 article "The Economic Consequences of the Dissolution of Cohabiting Unions," published in the *Journal of Marriage and Family.* This income loss is particularly pronounced for African-American and Hispanic women, with nearly half living below the poverty threshold at the end of a cohabitating relationship. The 2005 article is one of the first to document the changes in men's and women's economic well-being (including personal earnings, household income, income-to-needs ratio, and poverty) after they break up and are no longer living together.

Cohabitation has become commonplace in the United States, with the majority of young people having cohabited at least once. Most marriages now begin as cohabitations, according to article authors Dr. Sarah Avellar of Mathematica Policy Research, Inc., and Pamela J. Smock of the University of Michigan.

However, cohabitation is short-lived, with half of the arrangements lasting a year or less, the researchers found. Further, compared with previous decades, cohabitation is now more likely to end than lead to marriage, a change that is particularly pronounced for African-American women.

In post-cohabitation situations, after a breakup, a man's household income dips 10 percent, whereas women lose 33.1 percent. The percentage of women living in poverty increases from 20 percent to almost 30 percent.

By choosing cohabitation, couples are forgoing certain rights and protections provided for them in a marital union, according to the Equality in Marriage Institute, a nonprofit organization founded in 1998 by Lorna Jorgenson Wendt, who publicly battled her husband, former GE Capital Services chairman Gary Wendt. The institute was created by Wendt to help couples create, maintain, and, if necessary, dissolve their relationships fairly.

You can't live together and expect to automatically get the same financial protections afforded a couple who have married. Here's a typical cohabitation situation laid out in a letter I received from one woman who was about to move in with her boyfriend: "My partner makes less than half what I do, has no savings at age thirty-one, and lives from paycheck to paycheck. I am two years older, have a home, and significant savings. We are moving in together very soon, but I do not feel comfortable combining all our assets now or anytime in the foreseeable future until we are more settled. This is a constant cause of arguments because he feels we cannot grow together as a couple and truly trust each other if we don't share everything."

Oh, sure, this guy wants to pool everything. His woman has everything—a well-paying job, a house, significant savings. And what is he bringing to the table—a promise to live together?

Divorce laws set lots of rules when a marriage ends, but there's little legal protection for unmarried partners. Drawing up a cohabitation agreement or contract offers an unmarried couple only certain rights. A cohabitation agreement is a private contract between cohabitants, which typically tries to establish contractually for the parties the rights and obligations that married people obtain by state and federal statute. Without a cohabitation agreement, you and your ex-partner could face financial and legal chaos.

Before you draw up the cohabitation agreement, I suggest you read the Equality in Marriage Institute's booklet *The Commitment Conversation*. This guidebook walks you through a series of questions that includes lifestyle and financial issues. You can download a preview at www.equalityinmarriage.org.

Here's what the institute suggests should be in a cohabitation agreement, which you should have reviewed by an attorney:

- How property will be distributed if you break up. The agreement should cover all of your property, whether obtained during your time together or before. You should especially spell out who gets to keep what household assets. You may simply want to say that if you separate, each of you will have the right to take immediate possession of your separate property and that all jointly owned property will be divided equally. If there is property that you own together but not in equal shares, you'll want to specify a method for dividing it between the two of you.

- How expenses will be handled. Include details on who will pay for the day-to-day costs for food, utilities, laundry, housing, and other household expenses.

- How debts will be handled. If you have joint credit cards, how will those bills be divided if you split?

- How support, custody, or visitation rights for minor children will be handled (although in the case of children, you may still end up in court). If the guy you're moving in with is not the father of your children, will he still contribute to their care? All expectations should be spelled out.

- How health insurance coverage will be handled.

- How disputes will be resolved. Your cohabitation agreement should include a clause that stipulates the method of resolving disagreements.

- If you buy a house together, how will you handle ownership if the relationship fails? Who gets to stay? Will you sell and divide any profit?

You may be wondering if all this is really necessary. You bet it is. When you move in without the legal protections of marriage, you need to do more planning than deciding what curtains to hang. When the love goes, so can reasonability. Pay the money to hire an attorney to help you draw up a cohabitation agreement. It's important to have clarity about these financial decisions before you move in together.

## WHAT'S IN A TITLE?

During one online discussion, I received this question from a reader about her living situation: "My fiancé and I will be conducting some renovations to a condo he bought. We both live in the condo and we both will contribute to the cost of renovations. Currently, my name is not on the title of the condo, and as you know, cannot be added until we marry or he refinances the house. We will not marry for a year or so. Is there any way to protect my monetary contribution, even though my name is not on the title?"

Immediately, a few red flags went up for me. First, she will be spending her money to make major renovations to property she has absolutely no rights to. Second, I don't know what her fiancé may have told her, but she's dead wrong about the title situation. Her fiancé can add her to the title of the property anytime he wants. They don't have to be married, and he doesn't have to refinance the house to put her on the title. Could it be that he's lying to her, or just ignorant of the law?

So how can she protect her monetary contribution? Keep her money in her bank account until she gets married or her fiancé puts her name on the title of the condo.

Look at this advice from a family law attorney who joined the same online discussion: "I strongly affirm your advice to the woman who is living in a property owned by her fiancé and planning to make major financial contributions to his property. She seems to have a relationship issue brewing. He could put her name on the deed now, if he really wanted to. Please don't let your heart destroy your common sense. If they ever get married (she sounded shaky on that!), she had better stay on him to put her name on the condo, or better yet, sell it and buy something in both names. Marriage gives you property rights (why do you think the gay community is fighting for it?)—living together does not."

The situation the reader wrote to me about is very common. For example, one reader wrote: "My boyfriend and I have just moved in together. I have owned the house for five years. We have been dating for four years. He has no debt. I, on the other hand, have lots of debt. We're starting to buy things for my home and he has all these home improvement ideas, which I think are great, but I can't afford to do them now. He said he would pay for them because he wants the place to look nice. I'm not comfortable with this because we're not engaged (although we have plans on marrying someday). It's my house and I get all the tax benefits. I guess I don't want him to put all the money and work into it and not get any financial gain out of it. On the other hand, I just don't have any extra money to put into the house right now. I'll be digging myself out of debt for at least another two years. Should I let him go ahead and pay for the improvements?"

I told her the same thing I told the woman who was thinking of contributing to renovations on a house she doesn't own: Don't do it. Don't let your live-in boyfriend do it. And if he insists, then let him know up front that it's his choice; if you break up, the next guy will have a nicer place to call home.

### PROPERTY RIGHTS

If you're intent on buying property with a boyfriend, then make sure to spell out these points:

- Whatever money you put toward the closing costs, down payment, and loan fees, you must receive every cent back in the event that you break up.

- Will you both be on the mortgage? And if so, what happens if you want to leave and buy another house? Will he agree to refinance the house so that you can walk away from this debt?

- Will you both want to take the mortgage deduction? If so, you both need to be on the mortgage. (You can deduct home mortgage interest only if you meet several conditions, including being legally liable for the loan.)

- Be clear about what will happen if your boyfriend walks away from the house, leaving you with the mortgage. Who gets the house? Will you sell it?

Before you buy property with someone you are not married to, address all of these issues. And keep in mind that property held jointly is subject to claims by creditors of any of the owners. For example, suppose you add your boyfriend's name to the title of your home. Your boyfriend has a business that fails, and the IRS comes after him for unpaid taxes. Because he is now part owner of the house, the IRS may force a sale of the home. You will get a share of the proceeds, but you'll no longer have a home to live in.

Once you put your boyfriend's name on the title to your home, you have given him an ownership interest in your property. And that ownership right cannot be taken back without his permission. He would have to agree to what's called a "quitclaim."

A quitclaim deed allows a property's owner or co-owner to sign over all ownership and financial interests in a property. That said, if your boyfriend doesn't agree to a quitclaim, your only recourse might be to force a sale through the courts. Such legal action will come with a price—not to mention that you will have to fork over half the equity in your house.

If you are unmarried and plan to purchase a house with a boyfriend, get some legal advice from an attorney about the best way to hold title to the property. Here are the various ways property can be owned:

**Tenants in common:** Two or more people own property but without the right of survivorship. Each owner has a percentage interest in the property, typically fifty-fifty. However, such a split isn't mandatory. The percentage of ownership can vary. With tenants in common, if a co-owner dies, his or her interest passes to whoever is named in that person's will. If there is no will, state law will dictate which heir or heirs should get that person's share in the property. If you're a single mother or you have family members to whom you want to pass your share in the property, tenants in common is the best way to hold title to the property. If you do choose this option, be sure to have a will drawn up.

**Joint tenancy:** This is property owned by two or more people at the same time. Joint tenancy with the right of survivorship means that if one owner dies, the other assumes complete ownership of the property. The survivor takes all. It won't matter if the person has a will leaving the property to heirs. How the property is titled trumps the will. When the surviving joint tenant dies, his or her 100 percent title then passes according to the terms of the survivor's will or living trust.

**Community property:** This is a special form of joint tenancy between husband and wife. Each spouse owns one half of the property bought during the marriage. Both spouses can then will their share of the property to anyone they want.

**Tenancy by the entirety:** About half of the states recognize this special ownership right available to married people. Each spouse owns one half of the property. Neither spouse can sell the property or transfer ownership without the consent of the other. If one spouse dies, the other is entitled to the whole property.

If you're buying property with your boyfriend, the best way to title the property is as tenants in common.

# 9

—

# THE FINANCIAL RULES
# OF ENGAGEMENT

Once you move past the dating phase and decide to marry, it's time to change your financial relationship with your boyfriend. It's time to be as open with him about your money as you have been with your heart—and everything else, for that matter.

Once you get engaged, come clean about everything financial—your credit history, debt load, income, retirement plans. Discuss everything. It's vital that you exchange your views and values about money before you exchange wedding vows.

I know discussing money isn't always easy. Here's what happened to one reader who tried to talk to her boyfriend about their financial differences: "My boyfriend and I had a discussion recently about finances during a marriage. We have been dating a significant amount of time and things are getting serious. We're talking about getting married. Well, we found we have very different points of view on finances. My concern is that he became very upset that I felt differently from him and refused to compromise. Are these deep-seated beliefs able to be changed?"

Can someone change? Sure, but it won't be easy. That's why

you need to have the money conversation before you say "I do." Don't ignore the huge red flags waving in your face (he "refused to compromise"). If your fiancé won't even come to the table to talk, you have big problems. Communicate is the first of the three Cs in a relationship.

If your partner is shutting you down whenever you want to talk money, you have three choices. Stay and put up with the differences and the eventual conflicts. Walk. Or run for help.

If you want to stay, get help. Here's where you might turn to find counseling:

- Your church or religious organization. An increasing number of churches are offering premarital programs. Look for a program that includes a comprehensive session on money management that also covers the emotional issues about merging your money styles.

- Your benefits office at work. Many employee benefit packages include referrals to counseling services. You may find that your employee assistance program covers premarital counseling.

- Professional organizations. You can find a therapist in your area by contacting professional organizations for counseling. For example, more than fifteen thousand marriage and family therapists are listed on the website for the American Association for Marriage and Family Therapy (www.aamft.org). The Financial Recovery Counseling Institute specializes in helping individuals and couples with money issues. Demand is so high for such services that the institute provides financial counseling by telephone. In addition to dealing with the emotional issues about money, the institute teaches basic money management skills.

- A credit counseling agency. Often individuals seek help from such agencies for debt consolidation, but these organizations can also provide financial counseling. For an agency near you, go to www.debtadvice.org.

## TALK IS NOT CHEAP

If you want to try talking without counseling, you might wonder where to begin. Well, I've developed a quiz to get you started. After you've taken it, hand the book to your future spouse so he can take it, too. Then sit down during a nonstressful time and discuss your results. Make it a no-blame conversation. Communicate all your feelings. Don't hold anything back. Listen. Be patient.

 *Money Talks*

1. We have discussed how money was handled in each of our families.

    True

    False

2. I know exactly how much my future spouse earns.

    True

    False

3. I'm comfortable with how my future spouse spends his/her money.

    True

    False

4. I know how much he/she has saved in various saving and in-vestment accounts. We have shared these documents, too.
    True
    False

5. I know exactly how much debt my future spouse has.
    True
    False

6. We've talked about how the credit cards should be han-dled—if they should be paid off every month, or if it's okay to carry a balance.
    True
    False

7. I have seen all three of my future spouse's most recent credit reports and credit scores.
    True
    False

8. We have talked about how we each approach bill paying—for instance, I pay bills the day I get them; my partner always pays bills late.
    True
    False

9. My future spouse and I have discussed which one of us will handle paying the bills.
    True
    False

10. We've discussed whether we will talk about major purchases.
    True
    False

11. We have agreed to develop a budget.
    True
    False

12. We have discussed whether we will have joint or separate bank accounts.
    True
    False

13. We have discussed the possibility that one of us may want to be a stay-at-home parent and how that might impact our finances.
    True
    False

14. We have discussed our financial goals, such as buying a home or putting money away in a college fund if we have children.
    True
    False

15. We have discussed how much it would take for us to feel financially secure.
    True
    False

16. We have discussed and come to a compromise on how to deal with our different money styles—spendthrift versus cheapskate, for instance.
    True
    False

17. We have discussed whether it would be okay if either one of us quits his/her job to start a business, even if it means using our house as collateral for the start-up.
    True
    False

18. We have discussed the importance of meeting and discussing our finances regularly.
    True
    False

19. We have discussed how much we want to give to religious organizations or favorite charities.
    True
    False

20. We have discussed when each of us wants to retire and what type of retirement we envision.
    True
    False

How to Score: Add up the number of times you answered "True."

**20–18:** Go on to the chapel and get married. Unlike most couples, you have spent the time it takes to develop a plan that will help you live happily ever after financially.

**17–15:** You and your future spouse have a few areas where you might be tugging in different directions. But for the most part, you're doing okay. Still, be sure to address the questions that either of you answered with "False."

**14–10:** Don't make up the guest list for your wedding just yet. There are red flags all over your financial relationship. Clearly, you have a lot more talking to do before you take this engagement any further.

**9–0:** I hope you have the name of a good divorce attorney, because you're probably going to need one. You don't need to be discussing a wedding date. You need to be making a date with a financial counselor, because you're headed for some heated financial fights.

# 10

—

# THE MOST IMPORTANT PREMARITAL DOCUMENTS

Before you get your marriage license, you each need to get three important documents: all three of your credit reports from the major credit bureaus and all three (yes, you have three) of your credit scores. (I'll discuss these later in the chapter.) Once you have the reports and scores in hand, set up a time to swap them with each other.

When I suggest that couples share their credit reports, people often gasp. They giggle. They roll their eyes.

During one church-sponsored premarital counseling course I attended, the instructor began the personal finance session by telling the couples they would be required to exchange credit reports. Before this announcement, the couples had been joking and laughing. After it, they all fell silent. They stared at the counselors with looks that ranged from *No problem* to *Are you stark raving mad?*

"You love me, right?" one young woman asked her fiancé.

"Oh, Lord, I'll be waiting to see this," he answered.

Sharing credit reports is the most telling example of how each person handles money.

Think about it. Why would you feel uncomfortable sharing your credit report with the person you're engaged to? When you get married, you're going to be sharing every aspect of your life, so you shouldn't be embarrassed to show your loved one how you've managed your credit life, which can be key in getting insurance, a home loan, and even a job.

If you share reports, you will find out what one reader did: "My fiancé has a wrecked credit history. He has $18,000 plus [in debts] and he isn't working to pay it off because he's a student and has no money. I know he will, but for now there's a pile of letters from collection agencies. I've told him no marriage till his debts are gone. In the meantime, I'm not supporting him, either! I can't help but feel as if I'm being an ogre in some ways. Am I?"

I'll tell you what I told this woman. You're right to tell your man, *No romance without fixing your finances*. Too many couples start off their married life with an enormous amount of debt. That's a lot of financial pressure on a new marriage.

At least this reader found out about her fiancé's debt. I've heard from many women who are ashamed of their credit history. As a result, they hid it from their fiancés. When it comes to matters like this, don't lie. That includes lying by omission. The truth always comes out—often during a mortgage loan application. Is that really when you want your husband to find out you're tens of thousands of dollars in debt?

In addition, sharing credit reports will give you an opportunity to talk about premarital debt. With the reports and credit scores in hand, you can discuss what your expectation is if your loved one comes into the marriage with debt. For example, this reader asked: "If your spouse was a 'charge-aholic' before you got married, are you responsible for his debts after getting married? Can creditors attach commonly owned property?"

The answer to this woman's question is: It depends. In community property states, you could be held liable for debts your husband racked up as a single man. If you don't live in a community property state, you are liable for repayment of debts you both agreed to be responsible for—a cosigned mortgage, credit cards, a car note.

But let's look at this woman's question more carefully. She's aware that her fiancé has a credit issue and even calls him a "charge-aholic." She's worried about joint property being used to pay off debts he amassed when he was single. These are all red flags she shouldn't ignore. If she doesn't address this problem before she gets married, her new husband will take her down a dark debt road. And even if she isn't liable for his premarital debts, commonly held finances will be needed or diverted from other expenses to pay those bills. That's important enough that the two of them should be doing some serious talking about their finances.

As soon as you begin having discussions about getting married or right after you get engaged, order your credit reports. Set a date to talk about them. Debt happens to the best of us. Come to the table prepared to discuss, not argue or yell.

## WHERE TO GET YOUR CREDIT REPORTS AND SCORES

You need to get your credit reports from the three credit bureaus—Equifax, TransUnion, and Experian. Why all three? You need all three reports because each may contain different credit information. Each credit bureau keeps a separate file on you with information supplied by your creditors. Some creditors don't report consumer credit information to all three bureaus. So it's possible that what is on one report may not be on another.

The good news is, under the Fair and Accurate Credit Transactions Act of 2003, you are entitled to a free credit report from each credit bureau. Under the law, once every twelve months you can obtain a copy of your credit report *upon request*. There are several ways to get your free credit reports:

- Online at www.annualcreditreport.com.

- By phone. Call (877)322-8228. You will go through a verification process over the phone. Your reports will be mailed to you.

- By mail. You can request your credit report by filling out a request form (which you can find online) and mailing it to: Annual Credit Report Request Service, P.O. Box 105281, Atlanta, GA 30348-5281.

When ordering your credit reports, also request your credit scores (which are not free). You need all three scores because, just as with your credit report, each bureau generates a different score. You can go to the websites of each bureau to pay for your score.

The gold standard for credit scores is called a FICO score, named for the Fair Isaac Corp., based in San Rafael, California, which devised a mathematical model to predict the credit risk of consumers based on information in their credit reports. FICO is the credit-scoring model most widely used by lenders.

FICO scores range from 300 to 850. A score above 700 indicates that you are a relatively low credit risk and will likely qualify for the best interest rates. Consumers with scores below 600 are typically charged higher loan rates. Not only can a low credit score cost you thousands of dollars a year in additional finance charges, but you might also be denied insurance, telephone service, an apartment, or even a job.

All three major credit bureaus—Experian, TransUnion, and Equifax—use different scoring models, including FICO. When you order your credit score from the three bureaus, here's what you're getting:

- Equifax's credit score product is called "Score Power." Even though this uses the FICO scoring model, you may get a different score than one pulled by a lender because the information in your credit file is constantly changing. The score you get this week may not be the same score a lender would get from the credit reporting company the next week.

- Experian calls its credit score product "PLUS Score." It is based on factors similar to but not the same as FICO. The PLUS Score ranges from 330 to 830.

- TransUnion's credit score product is also not a FICO score, but is based on the bureau's own proprietary scoring model.

Although each bureau generates a different score, you need all three to get a complete picture of your creditworthiness. If you are about to be married, you should pull all six scores (three for you, three for your fiancé). The idea is to eliminate any nasty credit surprises.

## PRENUPTIAL PLEDGES

There's so much news in the press about prenuptial agreements that many couples just assume it's the norm these days. Here's a typical inquiry: "My girlfriend and I are discussing marriage. We are fortysomethings; no children and none expected; both working. I have meaningful assets and want a prenup and a basic understanding of how we intend to approach the economics of our partnership going forward. Hers would be a more traditional approach, less 'legalistic.' She feels my approach is atypical and could be perceived as 'insulting' as it somehow calls into question our trust. I wonder if you might comment on the increasingly common practice of prenups and how one approaches this in a way so as to minimize offense."

Would it surprise you that only 1 percent of Americans currently have prenuptial agreements with their spouse or fiancé(e)?

According to the American Academy of Matrimonial Lawyers, those couples who do have prenuptial agreements cite these reasons:

- A fear of divorce. No surprise there. Over the past several decades, divorce has become more prevalent, making a lifelong marriage less likely. There are now slightly more than one million divorces each year in the United States, compared with slightly more than two million marriages.

- A remarriage. There are increasingly more second and third marriages. People marrying for the second or third time say a prenuptial agreement provides clear guidance on what they are bringing into the marriage and what they expect to take out if things fall apart—again.

- Protection. Because they are marrying later in life when they have more assets, partners wish to protect themselves. For example, here's an online comment I received from one woman who wanted a prenup: "What if you are forty-plus, making a ton of money but spouse to be isn't and you don't want to be taken to the cleaners? Courtship ain't what it used to be. Guys don't woo you for a long time before you make the jump. Hell, you are practically expected to live together within a month. If there is an inequity in the finances, get a prenup." Another woman wrote: "I am thirty-one years old, single and with no kids. My net worth is more than $300,000. I have more than $150,000 in a 401(k), Roth IRA, IRA, CDs and index funds. I have about $200,000 in home equity. I would like to know how I can protect my assets in case I get married in the future."

- Distrust. Uncertainty about how courts will divide marital property. State courts are increasingly taking a broad view of marital property, including pensions, stock options, and even, in some cases, professional partnerships, such as law and medical practices. It is harder to make the case that assets you believe you have brought to a marriage should be considered separate from marital property. Academy members note that depending on jurisdiction, prenuptial agreements lose their effectiveness over time as more and more assets become marital property.

Still, do prenuptial agreements make smart financial sense or do they doom a marriage to fail? Americans are divided. At least that's the finding of one survey by Lawyers.com, an online consumer legal resource. The survey, conducted by market researchers Harris Interactive, found that 9 percent of unmarried Americans say they would not marry without a prenuptial agreement. Only 28 percent of those surveyed say prenups make smart financial sense for anyone getting married. Nineteen percent felt that a prenup is never needed when two people really love each other. Another 15 percent are convinced that a prenup dooms a marriage to fail.

I agree with the last two groups of people.

A prenuptial agreement is a plan to fail. Couples think such an agreement will make a breakup easier. Breaking up is *always* hard to do, whether you have joint accounts, separate accounts, or a prenuptial agreement.

Alas, I know this is a hard sell for some couples intent on protecting their stuff. Here's a comment I got from one reader during an online discussion about prenups: "I strongly disagree with your view of prenups as a 'plan to fail.' This is particularly so when folks get married later in life, with careers established and meaningful assets already accrued. That folks would want a prenup to establish how those assets are addressed in the event of a divorce strikes me not as a plan to fail but as good advance planning to avoid potentially nasty future disagreements. The reality is, about 50 percent of marriages end in divorce. Pretending it can't happen to me so I won't need a prenup is an ostrich strategy."

This reader is right. A prenuptial agreement is an advance battle plan.

But in a battle there are never any winners. A prenuptial agreement doesn't save marriages. It doesn't save couples from the nasty disagreements that come when the union dissolves. It often doesn't even prevent a court battle over assets. It says, *Honey, I don't really trust you, so let's lay out our exit strategy so I can take all my marbles—my money and my stuff—when I leave this marriage.*

### PRENUPTIAL PREPARATION

You may still think I've got my head in the sand, and so I begrudgingly offer this advice from the American Academy of Matrimonial Lawyers if you feel you must get a prenuptial agreement:

- You need to completely disclose all assets and liabilities. Failure to do so may invalidate the prenuptial contract.

- Each person should have his or her own attorney. Prenuptial agreements that are deemed excessively unfair to one party may be invalidated.

- There cannot be coercion, such as trying to get the person to sign the agreement the day before the wedding. Prenuptial agreements that appear to have been signed under pressure are more likely to be challenged in court.

- Be aware that state laws vary and can affect your prenuptial agreement. For instance, some states will not allow a waiver of alimony, viewing it as contrary to the public interest. Many states are adopting the Uniform Premarital Agreement Act. This act encourages the enforcement of prenuptial agreements by placing the burden of proving validity on the challenger and by limiting how deeply a court is allowed to look into the fairness of the terms of an agreement.

- Consider videotaping the agreement. Some prenuptials are videotaped to demonstrate that they were voluntarily signed.

# PART I: FIRST COMES LOVE

**What's the Bottom Line?**

Here's what you should have learned from part I:

✓ Women can't afford to wait for a man to plan for their financial future.

✓ Buy a home as soon as you can afford one—and you may be able to afford one sooner than you think. Don't wait for Mr. Right before taking this critical step.

✓ Likewise, start financial planning as soon as you can, including retirement, insurance, and estate planning.

✓ The first date is too soon and the honeymoon is too late to discuss personal finances. If you're still at the stage of dating just for fun and you're not really ready to settle down, keep your personal financial business just that—personal. But if you are ready for marriage, start talking.

✓ During the dating process is the time to ask the right financial questions: Does your boyfriend have to have the best of everything even though he isn't making a big salary? Is he living above his means? Is he a miser? Once you know the answers to these questions, you can honestly determine if you are willing to do what it takes to live in financial harmony.

✓ Figure out your financial deal breakers. It doesn't make sense to continue dating someone and fall in love with him if fundamentally you can't stand how he handles his money. Very few people can change their financial ways without a lot of hard work or counseling.

✓ Remember that the first C in a successful relationship is to communicate.

✓ If money is a motivation for your marriage, you'll have a bankrupt life. Besides, financial battles are fought by couples at every economic level—low income, middle income, upper income, and obscenely rich. It's how your man handles his money, not how much he makes, that can put you on the path to prosperity.

✓ Even if you decide to date your financial opposite, you can learn to compromise (remember, that's the second C)—but the compromising should come before the commitment to be a couple. And if you ignore the fact that you love to save and he loves to spend, you will be spending a lot of time fighting about money.

✓ If your boyfriend has some serious problems with his money, don't bail him out. Help him out by giving him the number of a good credit counseling agency. The same advice applies if you're the one in debt trouble. Handle your financial mess yourself.

✓ Don't cosign. When you cosign, you are on the hook for all of the debt.

✓ Don't get a joint credit card with your boyfriend. If you do, your credit could take some serious dings if he misses payments, pays late, or maxes out the card.

✓ Don't lend money you can't afford to lose.

✓ Don't think cohabitation makes the dissolution of your relationship financially easier. It doesn't. Unmarried couples face great difficulty establishing financial security for their partners and their families because many of the rules and regulations governing these areas are geared toward married couples.

✓ Once you get engaged, come clean about everything financial—your credit history, debt load, income, retirement plans. Discuss everything. It's vital that you exchange your views and values about money before you exchange wedding vows.

✓ Before you get married, you and your fiancé should share credit reports and credit scores.

PART TWO

THEN COMES
MARRIAGE

11
—

# GOING TO THE CHAPEL?
# DON'T COME OUT BROKE

One of the things I loved about my grandmother, Big Mama, was that she had what I call "financial integrity." Financial integrity is when you do only what you can afford to do.

If Big Mama couldn't afford to do something nonessential, she wouldn't stress about it. She wouldn't borrow to pay for it. She just accepted the fact that she was limited in the things she could do because she didn't earn much money as a hospital nursing assistant.

So when I decided to get married, Big Mama said, "Child, spend only what you can afford for a wedding because it makes no sense spending a whole lot of money for just one day."

I followed my grandmother's advice. I had a modest wedding that was paid for before we got back from the honeymoon (which we also didn't go into debt to fund).

However, couples (women) think nothing of borrowing upward of $30,000 for their "special day."

Every time I host an online chat about wedding budgeting or

speak to couples about this issue, I'm astounded at the amount of debt people want to rack up for their wedding. One woman asked me the following: "My father gave me a budget of $25,000 for my wedding but I am starting to think this isn't going to be enough. I was thinking of putting some of the smaller items— i.e., wedding party gifts, favors, and incidentals—on my credit card. My question is, how much debt is okay when paying for a wedding?"

Another woman asked: "If we are getting minimal help from our parents, is it foolish to finance most of our wedding through credit cards? I am not finding a whole lot of ways to cut costs and still have an elegant, classy wedding. We could use a credit card with perks, such as the GM card, and then put that toward a car in the future. What is your opinion?"

How much debt is okay when paying for a wedding? None! Weddings should be a cash affair—as in, all expenses should be paid with cash. If you use a credit card, make sure you pay off the bill in full. A wedding is a luxury, not a necessity. It's foolish to fund a wedding on a credit card.

I sat down with one engaged couple, Sharron and Frank, to talk about their wedding plans. Sharron wrote to me in response to a request that I sent out for couples with wedding-budget blues. "We will be financing the cost of our wedding without any assistance from our families," she told me. "I am paying for graduate school and we have just purchased a home together. As a result, we have depleted our savings. So, our dilemma is how to do our wedding on a budget."

I understand how so many couples might have the wedding-budget blues. In one survey, 43 percent of couples who got married said they spent more on their wedding than they had planned, according to Condé Nast Infobank, the wedding research arm of Condé Nast Bridal Group, publisher of *Brides* and

*Modern Bride* magazines. According to some research, the average cost for a wedding is about $22,000.

You might expect that I would immediately give Sharron and Frank advice on how to cut costs. For instance, buy a secondhand wedding gown. (I did.) Have a cash bar (did that, too). But in essence, I answered the couple's question with a question: "Have you two discussed your finances in detail?"

"A little bit," they said sheepishly.

You won't know how much to budget for your wedding if you haven't realistically looked at both your incomes and expenses.

Look at the actual numbers that make up your family balance sheet—what you own and what you owe. Once you've tallied up everything, it's time to identify your financial priorities. In Sharron and Frank's case, they wanted to put aside money for their graduate studies and get rid of some credit card debt.

After the couple identified their top financial goals, they concluded that they really didn't have a lot of money to spend on a wedding.

So how do you budget for a wedding? You might start with the calculator on www.weddingchannel.com. With the calculator (you will have to register to get access, but registration is free), you type in your projected budget and you'll get back an estimate on how much you should spend on your gown, flowers, cake, reception, and so forth based on national averages.

 **BRIDAL STATS**

American couples spend some $50 billion during their engagements on wedding attire, jewelry, beauty, and honeymoons. Below are bridal statistics, supplied by Fairchild Bridal Infobank, about the booming bridal business.

### Average costs of dressing the wedding party:

Bride's wedding dress: $790
Bride's headpiece/veil: $181
Other bridal accessories: $186
Day-of-wedding hair and
    makeup: $357
Bridal attendants' apparel:
    $735 (5 attendants)

Mother of bride's apparel: $236
Groom's formal wear (rented):
    $110
Formal wear for ushers, best
    man (rented): $575
    (5 attendants)

### Who pays for the wedding:

The bride's parents: 27 percent
The bride and groom:
    27 percent
Both sets of parents and the
    bride and groom: 15 percent

Both sets of parents only:
    7 percent
Other combinations:
    24 percent

## IS YOUR BIG DAY WORTH BIG DOLLARS?

Fast-forward ten years. What will you remember from your wedding?

If money is tight, stick with things that will have "memory value." Will you really care if you had crab puff appetizers? Will any of your guests remember what the wedding favor was? (How many of you have those little tiny bottles of sparkling cider under a cabinet collecting dust?)

Spend money for good wedding photographs. Those last. My three children love to pull out our wedding album and laugh at Mommy and Daddy smooching. But I doubt the wedding video will get much use. In fact, the fastest way to clear a room at a party is to offer to pop your wedding video into the VCR. And it can cost between $500 and $1,500.

My husband and I didn't bother renting a limo, which can cost about $600. Instead, my cousin drove us to both the wedding and the reception in his Jaguar. He even donned a top hat and served us sparkling cider.

I bought a used wedding dress from a secondhand store. I figured no one had to know it was used. Besides, only one other woman had worn the dress, and she wasn't going to be at my wedding.

I didn't have an open bar. People could go home and drink their own liquor.

Women, please. Have some financial integrity when setting your wedding budget. Figure out what is really going to make your day, and cut out anything else you can't afford—meaning you should make sure you can lay down cash rather than a credit card to pay for the affair.

After I wrote a column about the nonsense of spending tens of thousands of dollars on a wedding, I received a slew of mail from married couples who had advice for engaged couples.

"I had to write about these ridiculous wedding costs—$22,000?" one woman wrote. "What a down payment that would be for a first house. Or even a car bought outright, or college tuition. All of this to say . . . return to simplicity! Get married, don't put on a show."

Another reader said: "Setting a budget, developing common priorities, and agreeing on what is important for the wedding and subsequent household plans are the foundation for a good marriage."

I especially loved the advice from a woman who got married in 1969. Her mother offered her a choice: a wedding, or the money for a wedding.

"I chose the money and have been forever grateful," she wrote. "We started out with some money in the bank, rather than debt, and it enabled me to go on to professional school with a minimum loan. While wedding pictures and memories would have been nice, even nicer was the early financial security of a small nest egg. This is not the most fun or romantic approach, but I cannot praise its benefits enough. A wedding lasts a few hours. The money lasted years."

If you still would rather have a big shindig, however, here are some tips to cut costs:

Consider an unusual location (botanical garden, historic home) instead of a hotel. An upscale restaurant with a banquet room may charge $35 less per person than a catering hall. But be careful about selecting a nontraditional location: By the time you rent chairs, tables, china, and so on, the costs can add up.

Timing is everything, and that's especially true with a wedding. If you can, stay away from peak wedding booking times (May through October). You can also save money if you hold your reception on any night but Saturday. Saturday-night prices can be $20 more per guest than Tuesday night's, for example.

Seriously think about limiting your guest list unless you want to shell out some serious money (generally $7,600 for the average 168 guests). It's amazing how big the list can get. Many couples start out saying they want a modest-size wedding. But by the time the mamas and daddies add the must-invite relatives and friends, you're looking at a big wedding. Just say no.

Cut the number of attendants in the wedding. Couples have an average of ten attendants: five bridal attendants and five ushers, according to Condé Nast. A smaller wedding party means more money in your bank account (and fewer people to coordinate). You will also save on gifts for the attendants, which average about $500. And that's fewer people to feed at the rehearsal dinner (average cost, $875).

Cut your flower budget. Couples typically spend about $1,000 for flowers. For centerpieces, use potted plants such as baby rose plants or mini azaleas instead of cut flowers. Most important, select flowers that are in season—imported flowers can be costly.

Have the baker make a small wedding cake to display, photograph, and cut, and then have the waitstaff serve guests from a matching sheet cake that's kept out of view in the kitchen. You can purchase that cake from a grocery store or from a culinary school to save money. Nobody has to know it didn't come from a chic bakery.

If you feel you must serve alcohol, consider offering wine, beer, and soft drinks instead of a fully stocked bar, which can save $1,000 or more.

Here's an idea from a reader on how to save money on the wedding apparel, which on average costs more than $2,800, including the bride's gown: "We didn't have to spend a lot for our wedding clothes," the reader wrote. "There weren't any. We married in a nudist resort. What could be more memorable than that?"

Well, that's one way to save money, though I can't stand to see myself naked, so that wouldn't have been an option for me.

But just because this is your big day doesn't mean you have to go into big debt. As columnist Liz Smith said: "All weddings, except those with shotguns in evidence, are wonderful."

# 12

—

# GREEDILY EVER AFTER

On her wedding day, tradition says a bride should have something old, something new, something borrowed, and something blue.

Well, add to that something green—as in greenbacks.

There's a growing and disturbing trend among those heading to the chapel to get married. Many couples are asking that their wedding guests forgo buying them toasters, blenders, or china. Instead they are shamelessly and selfishly requesting cash and, more recently, stocks.

The more long-term-thinking couples want something blue other than what the bride might wear. That's blue-chip stocks. I've got nothing against giving stocks as a present. But asking for it is another matter. It's genteel panhandling, as far as I'm concerned, and not really very genteel. It's just plain tacky.

Increasingly, there are websites that allow couples to register for anything on up to a fully paid honeymoon. Couples are registering to have wedding guests contribute toward everything from hardwood floors to furniture, home down payments, computers, and even car payments.

Many cohabiting couples who register for stocks or creative gifts argue that they have everything they want for their home and don't need another candy dish, can opener, or coffeemaker. To these couples, I say: If you want to cruise the world on your honeymoon, more power to you, but do it on your own dime. If you want hardwood floors or a nice leather couch, save up for it yourself.

What's next? Will debt-laden newlyweds hand out their Visa account number and ask guests to help with their next credit card payment? Why not just cut out the registries altogether? The soon-to-be-wedded could just hand out their bank routing number and have guests electronically deposit money into their savings account.

I know there are many cultures where giving cash is acceptable and in some cases part of the wedding ritual. I don't have a problem with your mama, daddy, or a favorite auntie donating cash to help you pay for your wedding or honeymoon. But asking directly or indirectly for wedding guests to give you money to help pay for a car, a home, maid service, or a honeymoon is just being avaricious.

## I WANT WHAT I WANT

When I first snarled at the practice of asking for wedding presents in the form of money, expensive gifts, or stocks, the reaction from readers was passionate.

Some readers shared my distaste. Here's what one wrote: "I recently received an invitation to just gift the bride and groom with a check because their European honeymoon was being financed by MasterCard. They just signed a contract on a home, and were a little short on cash. What's next? An invitation to pay off the wedding couple's student loans?"

But other readers were fiercely supportive of this genteel pan-handling. I received a number of comments online, but I'll let this one, from a couple with student loan debt of more than a quarter million dollars, speak for itself:

"Our wedding was not lavish. [We] had about 140 people. Still, it cost $30,000. Add that, plus the ring and the honeymoon and other credit card debt, and we're now looking at $50,000 in short-term high-interest credit card debt. You might like to paint the picture of today's brides and grooms as money-grubbing yuppies with cash to spare, but in reality, most of us are struggling to pay our current bills and are throwing weddings for our friends and families far beyond our means. It is simply what is expected."

This couple is mad. First, a $30,000 wedding is not a modest affair. And if you're doing what is expected as opposed to what you can afford, you're mad. It's disturbing that this couple with $250,000 in student loan debt felt obligated to have an expensive wedding.

Contrary to popular belief, you do not have to live beyond your means. If potential guests expect you to go into debt so they can have filet mignon at your wedding reception, they aren't worth inviting.

What sense does it make to pile on more debt for a wedding and then moan and groan that someone was being thoughtless by giving you a waffle iron instead of cash to help you settle your debts?

New-age newlyweds argue that their needs should override the perceived tackiness of pleading with people to give them what they want. Why not just set up a cash register at the reception and charge admission to recoup costs?

Couples are not entitled to be compensated when they get married. A gift is an expression of affection, not a business transaction. As much as I know many couples need money, a wedding should not be used as an opportunity to hit up relatives and friends for money.

# 13

---

# TO MERGE OR
# NOT TO MERGE

When you marry, it's supposed to be about coming together as one. It's supposed to be about sharing, not trying to keep separate what you each bring into the marriage.

In Genesis 2:24, it says: "Therefore a man shall leave his father and mother and be joined to his wife, and they shall become one flesh."

There's no qualifier in that passage—"become one flesh." That means merging everything after marriage—your body, your goals, and, most important, your money.

Many couples complain that a joint bank account is akin to sharing a toothbrush—it can get nasty.

What nonsense. Keeping a joint account is not that hard. Deep down, couples who object to joint accounts really are objecting to the notion that they might actually have to communicate with their spouse about what they are spending or saving (or not saving).

I can tell that when couples ask if they should have separate accounts, what they really want is permission to set up a system they think will allow them to someday easily and harmoniously separate their assets.

Here's how I know. Read these typical questions submitted to me online by married women:

- "How should the bills be fairly divided?"

- "How is it fair that spouses contribute in proportion to their income? If one spouse works for more money, why should she have to contribute more and thus have less of her own money just because she's in a better-paying position?"

- "My husband and I contributed pretty much fifty-fifty to our bills since we made about equal amounts. I got laid off and I couldn't contribute to the bills. My husband has not said anything and is completely willing to pay my share until I get a new job, but suddenly I feel less of a partner in this marriage. Is this normal?"

- "I make nearly four times as much as my husband but feel like I never have money because I have to pay for the house, bills, car, and so on. Is there a fair way for him to contribute to the household expenses?"

Dig deep and all the questions revolve around one thing—fear. Fear that they're being taken advantage of. Fear that they will be abandoned with children and debt. Fear that they didn't realize they fell in love with a louse with no financial sense.

I'll be honest: I had the wrong attitude about how to handle marital assets. My attitude was that men couldn't be fully trusted so I needed to protect what I had worked so hard to earn. It's all that I knew.

The financial stability for our family was left to my grandmother Big Mama. Watching my grandmother struggle scarred me in many ways. I couldn't stand to watch her worry and fret about whether my alcoholic grandfather would make it home with his paycheck. I vowed in my early teens that I would be the master of my money. I would make it, spend it, and save it the way I wanted with minimum input from some man. My grandmother, based on her experiences, taught me not to be beholden to any man when it came to my money.

In fact, even after I got married, Big Mama continued to warn me about mixing all my money with my husband's. It's not that she wasn't pleased with my choice for a husband. She was. But she was scared for me. She just wanted me to protect my assets. "Child, you better keep you a little bank account on the side and don't let him know nothing about it," she advised.

I had planned to take Big Mama's advice.

My plan was to have seven bank accounts in my marriage—two that belonged to my husband (a savings and a checking account), two of my own (savings and checking), and a joint savings and joint checking account. The seventh account would be the secret "home-wrecking hussy account." You know, in case he ran off with some home-wrecking hussy.

I even had a plan for how I would be sure to clean out the joint accounts if my husband ever announced he was leaving me for another woman. I would fall to the floor in an emotional heap. There would be so many tears that I would go through a box of Kleenex. Then I would excuse myself to go to the bathroom, secretly taking the hands-free telephone with me. While in the bathroom, I would call up the bank and transfer all joint account funds to my secret account.

But thank goodness I met a man who understood what a marriage is supposed to be about. "If we get married, let's treat it like a partnership," he said while we were dating. "There is no yours or mine. It's all ours. The point is, we are a team."

My initial thought was *Team? Please*. Hadn't this man seen the divorce statistics?

However, under my husband's business plan for marriage, we would pool our resources. He felt that once the money was in one pot, we would be equally responsible to make sure it was wisely spent, saved, and invested. Separate accounts give you a back door, he said. With a back door, the theory is, you can walk out the door as you came in—with your own stuff.

My husband said there would be no back door in our marriage.

After numerous conversations, finger wagging, and a lot of neck and eye rolling on my part, I finally agreed to try it his way.

And you know what? My husband was right.

We got married in 1991, and we seldom have disagreements about money. When we do argue, it's usually about how much money I *won't* spend. That's because I'm so cheap that my husband has to enlist my girlfriends to take me shopping because I won't buy new clothes. If we need to buy a car, my husband has to start six months to a year in advance to persuade me it's time to push the older car off the road.

I'm blessed to have found my financial soul mate. We are both basically good money managers. But it's no accident that we rarely argue about money. We spent a lot of time before we were married getting to know each other's views and values on finances.

## PRACTICALLY SPEAKING, HOW DO YOU MERGE THE MONEY?

There are a few ways you can handle a joint account.

One method is that you both can carry a checkbook tied to a

joint account. This, of course, requires that you meticulously record all checks that are written. You may also need to frequently consult each other to ensure you don't accidentally overdraw the account.

If you are going to use this method, get overdraft protection. This is a service that banks offer to cover checks when you have insufficient funds in your account. A bounced-check fee can really sting—costing as much as $35. And a fee is usually charged on each check that bounces, even if several bounce in the same day.

Of course, overdraft protection comes with a cost. There could be a monthly or annual fee—or both. In addition, a transfer fee may be charged each day you trigger overdraft protection.

Here are three common types of overdraft protection:

1. Savings-linked. Under this plan, money is transferred from your savings account to cover an overdraft. Many banks do not charge a fee to link your savings account to your checking account. However, some do charge a monthly maintenance fee if your savings account dips below a minimum balance, which could happen when money is transferred to your checking account to cover bounced checks.

2. Line of credit. This is an unsecured loan to protect against bounced checks. The credit line sits unused until you need it to cover an overdraft. When you write a check or withdraw money from an ATM and there is not enough in your account to cover it, you get an automatic loan subject to the amount of your credit limit.

3. Credit card–linked. The bank links your checking account to your credit card and automatically charges a cash advance to your card to cover overdrafts.

Before signing up for overdraft protection, Consumer Action, a consumer advocacy group, recommends you get answers to the following questions:

• **What interest rate will I be charged?** Banks can charge anywhere from 7 percent to close to 22 percent for lines of credit linked to overdraft protection. Interest rates on the credit cards linked to overdraft protection can range from 9 percent to 20 percent.

• **How much is the transfer fee?** You are most likely to encounter transfer fees on overdraft protection linked to a credit card or a savings account. For credit card overdraft protection, transfer fees can range from $3 to $10 per day. For savings-linked overdrafts, transfer fees range from $5 to $10 per day. It's also possible you won't be charged at all.

• **Is there a minimum on each advance?** Overdraft advances vary by bank—some give you the exact amount; others advance cash in multiples of $100. If the bank lends only in multiples of $300, you would have to borrow $300 (and pay interest on it) even though you only need a few dollars to cover an overdraft.

• **Is there an annual fee?** Typically, banks don't charge an annual fee when the overdraft protection is linked to a credit card. However, many charge an annual fee for overdraft protection connected to a line of credit. Annual fees can range from $5 to $50.

• **How does paying off the overdraft work?** Just depositing more money in your checking account does not automatically cover the overdraft. It's important to pay back the overdraft specifically. Also, find out if the bank will automatically deduct a minimum payment from your checking account if you haven't made a payment on the outstanding overdraft balance by the due date.

While overdraft protection is useful to have, be careful you don't use it as a crutch to make ends meet.

If you're worried about bouncing checks, then limit your check writing. You can do that by paying your bills online. With online banking, you probably won't be able to eliminate all check writing, but if the two of you only have to write a few checks, you're less likely to bounce checks.

Another strategy for joint account keeping is to use a debit card instead of writing checks. Using a debit card frees you from carrying cash or a checkbook. Again, you need to record withdrawals so your spouse doesn't go to pay for lunch one day and discover there's no money. If you use a debit card, you should know there are two types of cards:

1. An online or direct debit card. With this type of debit card, money is immediately deducted from your bank account. To access your account at a store terminal, you have to key in your personal identification number (PIN), as you would at an ATM. The system checks your account to see if it has enough money available to cover the transaction.

2. An off-line debit card. This type of debit card looks like a credit card and its use resembles a credit card transaction. But unlike the online debit card, money from your account isn't automatically debited. It can take two to three days before the

money is electronically transferred (although you can't always count on that float). Instead of punching in your PIN number, you sign a receipt, just as you might for a credit card transaction.

Finally, to manage your joint expenses, you could use a credit card to pay for most of what you spend in the household during the month. I recommend this option only if you're extremely disciplined. You have to pay the bill off every month. With this option, you don't have to worry about bouncing checks. And the credit card statement is a good way to keep track of where the money goes during the month.

## HE COMES BEARING GIFTS

Often couples object to joint accounts because they can't figure out how to handle gift giving to one another. In some cases, couples will get three bank accounts to solve this one issue. They may have a joint account into which all moneys are deposited, and separate savings or checking accounts. Then they agree that each will get an allowance to be used as they see fit or to buy each other gifts.

I don't think all those accounts are necessary. So what if you know what your spouse spent on your birthday present? If you're the family's treasurer and you know your birthday or Valentine's Day or Christmas is coming up, don't peek at the online statement for that week.

The purpose of having a joint account is to give you both a full picture of the family finances. With separate accounts it becomes much easier for one spouse to keep a secret stash of money.

Having your finances joined also shines a light on possible overspending. If your spouse has his own bank account and you don't have any input into what he spends, how do you keep him from overspending? You can't even be sure when he overspends.

If you know your spouse will be looking over the joint checking account statement and credit card statements, you might be less inclined to go hog wild in your spending. The bottom line: Joint accounts promote accountability.

Once you marry, you are supposed to accept your husband as your lifetime mate. Of course, that's not always what happens. People get married and want to treat their husband as if he's a roommate and think all the bills have to be equally divvied.

Here's a typical question I get whenever I lead an online discussion about merging money after marriage: "My wife and I have been trying to figure out about how to decide how much we both should fairly contribute to our living expenses. My wife makes twice as much in salary as I do (her: $64,000, me: $34,000). How can we determine what is fair in our contribution toward our living expenses? If I tried to match half of everything I could not do it."

I'm sick and tired of hearing couples saying idiotic things such as, "He makes more than me so he should pay a bigger share of the utilities." Unfortunately, the new social norm is that when people get married, they do so thinking everything has to be equal, as if they are moving in with a roommate and they have to label all of their own food in the communal refrigerator.

With a roommate, there are *two* of you expecting to keep your stuff separate. The expectation is that someday you will go your separate ways—each leaving with the money and material things they brought into the relationship.

Merging your money with your husband is one way of getting rid of the *mine, mine, mine* attitude.

## TRUST BUT VERIFY

While it's important to trust your spouse, that doesn't mean you shouldn't keep tabs on what's going on. For all you know, he could be skimming money from your joint account. It's so common for spouses to trust too blindly.

You are making a big mistake by keeping out of the know about the family finances. Forget about whether your husband may run off with another woman, taking your money with him. What happens if he gets sick or, God forbid, he dies? Will you know what to do?

You may not like balancing the checkbook, but at least look through it. At least look at the monthly bank statement.

I like how one reader got her husband involved in the family finances. She wrote: "This is the situation I had with my husband. I was monitoring credit accounts and paying bills. But no matter what I did, I couldn't get him to understand how much money we were wasting (he's a spender, I'm a penny-pincher). Finally, I just let go for a couple of months. It was so hard, but I forced myself to be as financially irresponsible as I could, bought some things I'd been denying myself, ignored our finances, and when he asked about anything financially related, I shrugged my shoulders and said 'I don't know.' Basically, I acted as much like him as I could. And once he felt the impact of it, he started acting more financially responsible. He stopped spending so much. He does the bill paying with me. We discuss financial goals. The couple of months of being irresponsible cost us something in the short run, but has been well worth it in the long run. I finally feel like we're on the same financial team."

I hope you don't have to resort to such an extreme strategy—but hey, do what you can to ring loud bells for your spouse to get involved in the finances.

In a 2004 Quicken Personal Finance Study, nearly half of the respondents said their main problem with merging their money with their partner was a lack of control over the other's spending. Twelve percent of those who responded said they didn't want to share finances because of repeated questions about their spending.

Not sharing for these couples is a matter of control. Here's how one woman described her situation: "My hubby makes a decent living. But I make more. My question is, what gives him the right to decide how we spend it? Since I contribute most of the money, I think I should have the final say over whether he can go on a shopping spree to buy new clothes and scuba equipment."

What gives this woman the right to think she can lord over the family cash? Even though she's making more than her husband, she's not his mama. They are supposed to be a team. As such, if they treated all the money coming in as "theirs," there would be no need for her to think she needs to put her husband on an allowance as if he's a child. This is a case of domestic dictatorship, and it plays out in many a household depending on which spouse earns more.

Couples embrace this fifty-fifty nonsense and torture each other trying to come up with a formula to make sure everything is perfectly split. It's like when I cut slices of cake for my three children. Before they even take a bite, they compare how big a piece their siblings got. But in life, just as in cutting up a cake, you can't always make it equal. Somebody may in fact get a bigger slice—this time. But eventually things even out. The next time the cake is sliced, you may get the bigger piece. Everything does not have to be equal to be fair. If couples stop acting as if they were children, they could see that merging their lives and their finances can work without a lot of fussing and fighting. Sure, they might still have disagreements, but they don't have to let them end in land-mine-filled battles.

By joining forces and keeping finances together rather than

separate, couples can learn to lean on each other—using the financial strengths each brings to the marriage. For example, if one spouse is frugal, that person can help the other become less of a spendthrift. On the other hand, the frugal spouse can be taught to loosen up a little and have some fun.

"My overspending would not have been tempered if I had not married my husband," one premarital financial counselor told me. "I push him to spend and he pushes me to live within a budget. As long as your finances are separate, you're not capitalizing on each other's strengths. If you want to be savvy money managers, it's going to take both your sets of financial skills."

When you get married, it's not about you anymore. "You" cease to exist. Your life is now about the two of "you." So stop fighting about how your paychecks should be allocated so you can be sure to keep what is yours. If you bring your funds into one pot, it doesn't matter who makes more. You don't have to fight about apportioning the bills so that everything is "fair."

If you had joint accounts and you both truly believed that what comes into the house belongs to both of you, then this wouldn't be an issue. So pool your funds. And remember, he's your husband, not your child. You don't need to be a domestic dictator to settle this issue.

The reward to having joint accounts is that you can rejoice in each other's financial accomplishments because they belong to both of you. Look at how this husband viewed his wife's boost in salary: "I helped put my wife through law school on a public interest salary. Now she is a partner in a law firm, making $200,000. All I have to say is YIPPEE!! While my salary has increased significantly too, she will always make much more than me unless I switch to corporate work. Marriage is about making it possible for both of us to pursue our dreams. It does not matter which of you makes more money as long as you both are free to achieve your goals."

# 14

---

# HOUSE RULES

In 1981, 4 million wives made more than their husbands, according to the U.S. Census Bureau. By 2001, that number had more than doubled to 8.1 million.

Once you've taken my Money Talks quiz (page 67), it's time to develop what I call House Rules. It's imperative that you establish a set of guidelines to govern how you will deal with money in your household.

Think about it. We work for organizations that have rules on how we are to conduct ourselves in the workplace. And yet when it comes to our personal lives, we rarely establish written rules of engagement.

For example, my husband and I have rules for just about every aspect of our home life. We even have a rule on how to conduct ourselves during an argument. When we are arguing, neither of us can bring up past incidents. If the rule is violated, we get "buzzed." Let's say I'm fussing at my husband for dropping his shoes in the middle of the family room. If I complain about it, he can't bring up at that moment a time when I may have done the same thing. If he does, I make a buzzing sound to indicate he has violated the rule.

The buzzing accomplishes two things. First, you make your husband aware that he's veering away from the issue at hand and trying to shift the focus from his own act. Second, it brings levity to the situation, since the buzzing is both annoying and funny.

Establishing House Rules has worked wonders for us. We have civil, respectful disagreements. The key is for both of you to buy into the concept that the rules are a mandate. They can't be changed unless you both agree.

Here are some financial House Rules you may want to consider adopting as your own:

- "We agree that neither of us can make a purchase of $200 or more without first consulting the other." The point of this rule is to get you to discuss your spending. Even if you both keep separate accounts, it's important to talk about your joint and separate expenditures.

- "We agree that in the case of a major purchase, both of us must vote in the affirmative. If either one of us says no, the deal is dead." Some of the biggest arguments over money result when one partner wants to spend money on something the other doesn't approve of. I have heard from spouses furious that their partners made major purchases (house, car, big pieces of furniture) without their approval or against their wishes. This can cause a major breach of trust in the relationship—not to mention a financial strain. For example, let's say your husband decides he wants a luxury SUV that will end up costing $700 a month for five years. Your husband may argue that the car note is coming out of his check and therefore you don't have a say in the decision. However,

such a hefty car payment may mean he needs to work over-
time or get a second job. Now, tell me how that purchase will
not affect the family! Clearly, it should have been jointly decided. I'll admit that this rule does have its downside. In my
house, it takes almost a Geneva-type summit to buy furniture or to select carpeting. But the result is that nobody is
bullied into buying something that they don't want or that
they feel would be a huge financial mistake.

- "We agree there will be no financial secrets. No secret bank
accounts. No earnings that are not disclosed." Again, even if
you decided to keep separate bank accounts, you should
make full financial disclosure a hard-and-fast rule in your
house. Think of it this way: When two businesses merge,
there is complete disclosure of all assets. There is always a vet-
ting period when the two companies open their books completely. The same should be the case for your marriage.

- "We both pledge to establish a plan to meet regularly to discuss the family's finances."

- "We agree to operate under a budget and agree to adhere to
it." In chapter 16, I'll discuss how to set up a budget, so you
may have to come back to this rule to work out the details.
Essentially, the point of this rule is to get you both to establish upper limits on certain line items. For example, the two
of you may agree that neither of you will spend more than
$75 for a pair of sneakers for the children nor more than $50
for their birthday gifts in one year. If limits are set and followed, you don't have to worry that when your partner is
shopping, he'll go overboard and sabotage the budget.

- "We agree that one of us will be designated as the money
manager in the household." I could advise you to switch off

handling the bills, but realistically that generally doesn't happen. One spouse typically ends up being the family's treasurer. That's okay. At the very least, review the finances at least once a month.

- "We agree there will be no financial tit for tat." I have seen countless couples try to outspend each other in the name of fairness. For instance, my husband plays golf. Golfing is an expensive hobby. I love to read and play Scrabble. What I spend on books in a year doesn't come close to what he spends in a year to golf. But I don't try to go out and spend money on other things to equal his spending. That would just be childish.

- "We agree that all discussions about our finances will be conducted in a respectful manner. We will not cuss at each other. We will not degrade each other. We will not yell at each other. If either of us breaks one of our House Rules, we will own up to the digression and find a way to prevent it from happening again."

This all may seem too formal to you—even businesslike—but if you want financial peace in your household, you must develop a set of rules to govern your financial behavior. Will the rules be broken? Sure they will. But having them as a baseline of how to conduct yourself will help you quickly get back on track.

# 15

---

# WHAT WE HAVE HERE IS
# A FAILURE TO COMPROMISE

Throughout the book, I've been talking about the three Cs. The second C is probably the hardest to do, especially if you're a woman who is older and who has most of what she needs.

Compromise for many women is scary. They see it as giving in or giving up what they want. Take, for example, an online question I received from one engaged woman. She and her fiancé each had a home. She wanted to keep her ninety-year-old row house. Her fiancé wanted them to live in his house in the suburbs.

She wrote: "His house is a better size for us but its location is not as good as my home. This has caused innumerable frustrating conversations between us. We cannot seem to come to a resolution. Can you shed any light on this situation or provide any advice?"

When you get married, it's no longer about what you want. In the case of the two-house couple, the compromise is simple—sell. Is the house she's living in now more important than finding a *home* she and her new husband can both enjoy? If you were in a similar situation, would you really want your husband to move into your house and be so unhappy that it caused arguments all the time? It's just property. You can learn to love another house. But do you want to learn to love another man?

When you get married, it's not all about your wants anymore. Marriage means compromising. And when you compromise, it doesn't mean there are two losers.

# 16

## WHAT WE HAVE HERE IS A FAILURE TO SET COMMON GOALS

Considering how often couples have disputes about money, I was actually surprised to find out that most couples make lots of shared purchase decisions, especially about big-ticket items.

According to a survey by RoperASW, a national marketing and research company, an overwhelming majority of married men and women say that financial decisions about vacations, savings, investments, and cars are largely joint ones, with equal input from both spouses.

If you handle your purchasing decisions this way, good for you. That's how it should be. To do otherwise is to create problems.

The survey also found that with everyday purchases such as food, cleaning products, personal care products, and over-the-counter drugs, women usually decide what and how much to buy.

"This means more of the burden of the day-to-day running of the household falls to women, even as more and more women are working," said Ed Keller, chief executive for RoperASW.

However, minor purchases can cause mighty big arguments, too. "I often hear couples argue over whose budget is this coming out of," said Catherine Williams, vice president of financial literacy for Money Management International, a consumer credit counseling service. "You need to set up a system for purchasing everyday items."

I can't tell you how many husbands I've heard complaining because their wives spend too much money on clothes for the children. Or that every time they turn around, there's a new kitchen appliance or piece of household furnishing. And then there are the wives who complain that their husbands spend too much on computer software or electronic gadgets.

You don't have to call your husband from the grocery store and ask which brand of peanut butter you should buy. But for small things, it's important that you agree on how much you will spend in each expense category.

> **"Beware of small expenses because a small leak can sink a big ship."**
>
> **Benjamin Franklin**

It's easy to forget the small things if you're focused just on the big stuff. So you know what that means. Yes, creating a budget.

And don't roll your eyes. At least I'm consistent. *Budget* is not a bad word. It's an essential tool for everyone, most important, couples. You don't have to come up with an elaborate spreadsheet. If nothing else, you should have price guidelines for major and minor purchases.

RoperASW conducted its survey to help retailers tailor their marketing campaigns. But I think married consumers can use the survey results as a reminder that they do have to sweat the small stuff.

If you want to know whether you share the same common financial goals, take this test put together by the Texas Society of Certified Public Accountants.

## Compatibility Quiz*

**1. How often do you and your significant other or spouse discuss your financial situation?**
- **A.** Once a week.
- **B.** Once a month.
- **C.** Once a year.
- **D.** Never.

**2. Have you set a monthly budget or plan to guide your spending?**
- **A.** Yes.
- **B.** No.
- **C.** Don't know.
- **D.** What's the point? We don't have any money.

**3. How have you divided the financial responsibilities in your household?**
- **A.** One takes care of everything. The other is oblivious.
- **B.** One pays bills, while the other tracks investments and insurance coverage.
- **C.** We sit down together and do everything as a couple.
- **D.** Nobody takes responsibility for financial matters.

**4. If you receive a bonus or an unexpected windfall, how would you spend your money?**
- **A.** Immediately head to the mall for an afternoon of self-indulgence.

*Reprinted with the permission of the Texas Society of Certified Public Accountants.

**B.** Pay down mutual debt.

**C.** Save a little, spend a lot.

**D.** Contribute to an individual retirement account.

### 5. Have you ever tried to disguise or hide a purchase from your significant other or spouse?

**A.** No, I'm always honest.

**B.** Maybe once or twice.

**C.** Only around the holidays.

**D.** Regularly.

### 6. How much money would you feel comfortable spending on a single purchase without first conferring with your significant other or spouse?

**A.** Less than $50.

**B.** $51–$100.

**C.** More than $200.

**D.** I don't see any reason to check with my spouse before spending money.

### 7. If you want to make a major purchase as a couple, what do you do?

**A.** Open up a store charge card, or charge it on the card with the most room.

**B.** Save the amount needed before making the purchase.

**C.** Take the money out of savings.

**D.** Resist the temptation, and make do with what we have.

### 8. How do you plan to teach your children about money responsibilities?

**A.** An allowance system where children earn money for completing their chores each week.

**B.** We regularly give our children money to buy whatever they want, because we want to be generous with our money.

**C.** We try to set a good example for our children, and we expect them to follow our lead.

**D.** We talk about spending, saving, and investing with our children.

## 9. Have you made provisions to care for your significant other or spouse in case of death or disability?

**A.** Yes. I have an updated will along with disability and life insurance policies.

**B.** Yes. I made a will ten years ago.

**C.** No. I'm too young for anything bad to happen.

**D.** No. My significant other or spouse knows how I would want my property and possessions divided.

## 10. Are you and your significant other or spouse actively saving for retirement?

**A.** No, we hope to use our family inheritances for retirement.

**B.** No, we don't have any money to spare.

**C.** Yes, we regularly set aside money for retirement.

**D.** Yes, we have mapped out a retirement savings strategy and follow the plan.

Now compare your answers with your spouse's, and see if you're on the same financial page.

> If you had the same answers to at least eight of the ten questions, then you are two peas in a pod. Your relationship seems to be rock solid, at least in the finance department.

> If you had the same answers for more than five questions but fewer than eight, your financial relationship needs some

work. You're headed in the right direction, but you need to check the couple compass before making your next financial move.

If you answered fewer than five questions the same way, then you and your spouse may need to set some common goals. You're clearly at opposite ends of the financial spectrum, and you'll need to close that gap if you want to reach your financial goals.

These types of questions can help frame your future financial discussions and develop goals for your joint future. Check http://www.valueyourmoney.org for online tips from CPAs to help you address the financial issues raised in this quiz.

## BUDGET IS NOT A BAD WORD

> **"A budget takes the fun out of money."**
>
> **Mason Cooley**

Some people think a budget means they have to live an austere life. In fact, in an effort to get people to budget, some experts say don't call it a "budget" at all. Instead, they advise, call it a "spending plan."

The name change is intended to make you feel better. It's supposed to put the focus on the fact that you can still spend on a budget. If it makes you feel better, call your budget a spending plan. Call it a "financial blueprint," or call it whatever it takes to get you to figure out how much money you have coming in and how much is going out, because that's all a budget really is.

Budgeting is like starting out on a road trip to an unfamiliar location. You can guess how long it will take you to get to your destination and which routes to take, but you'll probably get lost, be late, or maybe never arrive. If you plan your trip, though, you'll know precisely what it takes to get from point A to point B. Same with saving.

You've got to plan so you know where you are going, and that means a budget.

"Most people have it all wrong about wealth in America," Thomas J. Stanley and William D. Danko wrote in *The Millionaire Next Door*. "Wealth is not the same as income. If you make a good income each year and spend it all, you are not getting wealthier. You are just living high. Wealth is what you accumulate, not what you spend."

If you want to accumulate wealth and not debt, think of your finances as a pyramid. The foundation of your financial pyramid should include an emergency fund of three to six months of living expenses. Next, make sure you have enough life, health, and disability insurance. Before building that pyramid any higher, pay off your high-interest consumer debt, such as your credit card bills. If you are too deep in debt to see a way out, you may need help from a credit counseling organization.

Once you've got a handle on your debts, the rest of your pyramid should be investment-oriented. Plan for short-, medium-, and long-term goals, such as saving for a car, a house, college education for your children, and your retirement.

Most important, take advantage of tax-deferred savings plans offered by your employer. If your company provides a matching contribution to your retirement savings plan, do what you have to do to qualify for all that money (eat in, skip a couple of movies, cancel cable). If you don't, look at what you could lose:

Let's say you earn $50,000 and your company will match contributions to your 401(k) plan, dollar for dollar, up to 6 percent of your total income. The maximum amount that can be contributed on a pretax basis to a 401(k) or 403(b) plan is $15,000.

But you decide to contribute only $500 a year to your plan. The company matches your contribution, giving you another $500. Had you contributed the maximum 6 percent, however, you could have gotten an additional $2,500 from your employer. Now consider the power of compounding. That $2,500 at 8 percent could grow to $39,114 over ten years, or $123,557 in twenty years. And you'll be saving an equal amount of your own money—all tax-deferred.

Think about it. You are leaving some serious money on the table.

As you build your pyramid, make it your primary goal to become better informed. Included in this book is an appendix listing a number of websites that will provide you with further information on mutual funds, stocks and bonds, estate planning, finding a financial planner, and common investment scams.

As Benjamin Franklin wrote, "An investment in knowledge always pays the best interest."

## SAMPLE BUDGET (SPENDING FOR SUCCESS)

### *Major Items to Include in Your Budget*

• **Income:** Enter any and all disposable income you receive from paychecks, interest, investments, alimony, child support, Mom and Dad, and so forth. This is your take-home pay.

• **Household Expenses:** The household category is designed to make your budget easy to manage by lumping many items into one category. List all expenses you have between paydays. Try to keep this item to no more than 30 percent of your gross income. If you want to calculate what you have to earn to keep your housing expenses affordable—or no more than 30 percent of your income—go to www.nlihc.org/oor2003/calc.php.

• **Transportation:** If you have a car, the name of this game is to get the cheapest car possible. Buy used. Don't lease.

• **Credit cards:** You will notice there is no line item for credit cards. You used those cards to buy something, so specify in your budget what you charged on your card. Remember, you are using other people's money. You are buying stuff with money you don't have and aren't sure you're going to have next month—otherwise you would have paid cash for it!

• **Savings:** This is possibly the most important of all the categories. It is absolutely necessary that you make plans for your financial future and put money away to pay for it. Your short-term savings (crisis fund) are used to cover unexpected and irregular expenses. Your long-term savings will allow you to fulfill your ultimate long-range goals (paying off your credit cards, college education for your children, buying a home, a secure retirement). You should always save at least 10 percent of your income. How you divide it between long- and short-term savings is up to you, although a fifty-fifty split seems to work best. If you believe in tithing, you will have to save 20 percent of your income.

• **Giving:** Be sure to build giving into your monthly budget. Make it as important as paying your mortgage or rent.

## THE BUDGET WORKSHEET TO MATCH
## YOUR EXPENSES WITH YOUR INCOME

| *Income + Expenses* | Estimate | Actual |
|---|---|---|
| Monthly gross income (what you wish you could keep!) | $_____ | $_____ |
| Monthly net income (the pitiful amount you actually take home) | $_____ | $_____ |
| Tithes or charitable giving | $_____ | $_____ |
| Rent/mortgage | $_____ | $_____ |
| Household Expenses | | |
|    Utilities: | | |
|    Gas/oil | $_____ | $_____ |
|    Electric | $_____ | $_____ |
|    Water | $_____ | $_____ |
|    Telephone (including cell phone) | $_____ | $_____ |
|    Internet access | $_____ | $_____ |
|    Cable | $_____ | $_____ |
|    Groceries: | | |
|    Food | $_____ | $_____ |
|    Household supplies | $_____ | $_____ |

Transportation

    Subway/bus          $_____     $_____

    Gasoline            $_____     $_____

    Car payment (you'd better
    not be leasing unless it's
    a business expense)      $_____     $_____

    Car maintenance (get a
    roadside assistance plan)   $_____     $_____

Extracurricular supplies or
fees for children         $_____     $_____

Insurance:

    Home               $_____     $_____

    Health             $_____     $_____

    Life                 $_____     $_____

    Auto               $_____     $_____

    Other (disability, long-
    term care)            $_____     $_____

Entertainment:

    Meals away from home     $_____     $_____

    Movies/concerts/theaters   $_____     $_____

Health club, etc.         $_____     $_____

Vacations             $_____     $_____

Personal:

   Clothes                                      $_____  $_____

   Grooming (e.g., haircut)       $_____  $_____

   Other_____        $_____  $_____

Miscellaneous (specify):

   Loans to friends or family
   members                                   $_____  $_____

   _____  $_____  $_____

   _____  $_____  $_____

   _____  $_____  $_____

Total income                                  $_____  $_____

Total expenses                              $_____  $_____

Monthly surplus/deficit                $_____  $_____

How much extra you need
monthly in case of a deficit (get
another job or *cut expenses*)     $_____  $_____

## YOUR MONEY, YOUR MAN, AND YOUR BUDGET

### Have a Plan

Without a definite plan of attack, your budget goals will probably
be doomed. Like diets, many of us have started on family budgets

only to see them wither away with time. If you are like most of us, you will probably need a program that has some structure but won't force you to turn your life inside out.

### Pay Yourself Before You Pay Everybody and Their Mama

Both of you need to decide how much you want to put aside from every paycheck every single time you get paid. If you wait until after you pay your bills, you won't save. Set up an automatic way for money to go directly into your savings account. Follow this rule and you will begin to have more money.

### Gather Records

The process of developing and maintaining your budget is much simpler if you have the records of your current spending on hand. Rather than saying, "I think I spend about $200 a month on groceries," you will have the exact average monthly expenditures for various items. Keep track of receipts from utilities, physicians, service stations, and any expense that varies from month to month. Once you have a running total for several months, you can develop an average and adjust your budget up or down accordingly.

### Actualize Your Goals

A budget is only as good as the goals attached to it. For example, you may decide that you want to get rid of your credit card debt. But it's not enough to just say that. Figure out how much you need to put toward that debt each month. Start slowly with a fairly easily attainable goal and then "test" yourself with a more difficult (and rewarding) goal as you get more proficient at your budgeting process.

For example, let's say you have charged a total of $1,500 on your credit card. If your minimum payment each month was $30 on a card with 19.9 percent interest, it would take you more than twenty-five years to pay off your debt! Even worse, you would end up paying a total of $6,000—even though you borrowed only $1,500.

If you doubled what you pay each month to $60, then it would take only two and a half years to pay off your debt, and you'd pay only $1,900.

### Where to Keep Your Emergency Money

A nationwide survey by the Consumer Federation of America and Visa USA found that a lack of personal savings to cover periodic emergency expenditures was a principal cause for financial worry among women, especially younger women. This has resulted in sleep and job productivity loss as well as health problems.

Forty-two percent of all women surveyed said they had emergency savings of less than $500.

A large majority of the unexpected expenses that women worry about are related to health care (36 percent) or transportation (32 percent)—their cars. Now, do you drive a car? Have you ever known a car *not* to need something fixed eventually? A car repair should not be an unexpected expense.

One of the key things you need to do to build a sound financial house is to stash away enough money so that you can cover living expenses for at least three to six months. But how do you calculate how much emergency money to set aside, and where should you put it?

Determining how much you need will take a little financial figuring. This means pulling out your bank and credit card statements. With these in hand, start calculating how much you spend each month. How much is your rent or mortgage? On average, what do you spend for food? What does it cost you to go to work each month? What does it take to fill your car's gas tank every week? Don't forget about day care expenses or insurance payments (car, life, home, disability). Most important, be realistic about what you pay out every month to make ends meet.

Now take that amount and multiply it by three or six to get the amount you should have as an emergency fund.

The next thing to figure out is where to park the money until you need it. Keep in mind that this is money you want to keep liquid—meaning you can get your hands on it quickly without having to sell something or pay an early-withdrawal penalty. (That might happen if you lock this money up in a long-term certificate of deposit.) This isn't money you are "investing." Your mission here is to protect your principal.

Here are some options:

• **Savings accounts:** I know that rates on deposit savings accounts can be extremely low. But a savings account is one of the safest places to put your emergency or living-expenses money. I keep my if-I-lose-my-job money in a credit union account. This money is automatically deducted from my paycheck. My credit union has very few branches, so I can't get my hands on the money for quick cash to pay for a trip to the dry cleaners or the grocery store. I also don't carry the ATM card attached to this account. These are all obstacles I put in place to ensure I'm not tempted to dip into this money.

• **Certificates of deposit (CDs):** Unfortunately, rates for short-term CDs are also pitiful. But you could "ladder" your CDs. CD laddering allows you to take advantage of typically higher rates offered by longer-term CDs while maintaining access to some of your money. Instead of buying a five-year CD, you might divide your money into equal portions and buy a series of CDs that mature at different times. For this purpose, you could buy CDs that mature in six months and one, three, and five years. That way you don't have to tie all your money up in lower-paying CDs. Bank of America has an online calculator to make the process of CD laddering a little easier. Go to www.bankofamerica.com and search for "CD laddering." The online tool calculates how much will be earned under certain laddering scenarios using the bank's current CD rates and annual percentage yields (APYs). You don't have to buy your CDs from this bank, but I found the calculator very easy to use.

• **Money market deposit accounts:** These are interest-earning savings accounts offered by FDIC-insured financial institutions. Money market deposit accounts offer many of the same privileges as checking accounts. But you are limited in the number of transactions you can make. No more than six transfer or withdrawal transactions may be made in one month, and of those six, no more than three checks may clear in one month. Money market accounts also have a minimum balance requirement. Check around for rates. Try www.bankrate.com. Additionally, Bankrate .com suggests that you ask these questions before opening a money market account: What is the minimum opening deposit? Is there a monthly maintenance fee? What's the fee for writing more than three checks a month? Is there a fee if my balance drops below the required minimum? Can I get a higher interest rate if I deposit a larger amount?

• **Money market mutual fund accounts:** These are quite different from money market deposit accounts. Money placed in this type of account is not federally insured. When you invest in these funds, your principal is not guaranteed. But the risk of losing your principal is extremely low. You can sell your shares in a mutual fund at any time, and many have check-writing privileges (with limits, of course). Money market mutual funds usually invest in Treasury bills, bank CDs, and high-rated corporate bonds. Usually this account will pay higher interest than a bank money market account and respond faster to a rise in interest rates. Still, the rates on these accounts aren't great right now, so shop around.

I know that for many, it's not easy to save several months' worth of living expenses. But you don't want to be caught without some money saved to carry you through a rough financial period.

# 17

## WHAT WE HAVE HERE IS A FAILURE TO COMMUNICATE

In a marriage, financial honesty is right up there with fidelity. And yet men (and women) think nothing of keeping financial secrets.

Look at one reader's plight. She wrote: "I've been married for two years, and I'm at my wit's end. My husband, while a bright and caring husband and physician, is completely irresponsible with money. He has obtained numerous credit cards without telling me, and has the bills sent to his mother's house (I found out when his mom forwarded the bills to our house). I find hidden purchases all over the house, or he tries to pass off brand-new stuff (a $1,200 PDA) as something he's always had. We've talked about this endlessly, and seen two marriage counselors. He promises to change and then just goes back to his secretive and expensive ways. He is a good man, but I'm wondering at what point I should just give up on this marriage."

Honestly, as I told this reader, a good man wouldn't lie to his wife. Nor would a good woman lie to her husband.

A woman often hides her money from her husband just in case he turns out to be a philanderer, spendthrift, or financial control freak. There are experts who advise women, especially stay-at-home moms, to keep a separate stash of cash. They even provide tips on how to carry out the deception. Here are just a few:

- When you go to the grocery store, write a check for an amount over the total and hoard the cash you get back.

- Secretly sell off odds and ends around your home at swap meets, flea markets, and garage sales.

- Find a part-time job that will pay you in cash.

- Open a non-interest-bearing account in your maiden name in another city. Make sure all bank statements are sent to a secret post office box.

Almost anything goes to protect your money. Women are told not to feel guilty about hiding money so they can shop without having to justify purchases, or invest without their husbands' knowledge, or raise cash for a rainy day.

After all, it's about time that women—who are increasingly earning more than their husbands and bringing more assets into a marriage—learn to conceal their true financial situation the way some men do.

I hear it all the time. Women should strive to maintain as much financial independence as they can. Experts advise women to keep separate accounts and sign up for credit cards in their own name just in case they get divorced. Fail to do so, they warn, and you may have trouble getting credit after the marriage ends.

I know many women who harbor fears that their husbands will have affairs and clean out their bank accounts. It would be foolish not to protect your financial interests at a time when so many marriages end in divorce.

But that fear, however realistic it may turn out to be, does not justify dishonesty. It's possible to have financial independence without being deceitful. A marriage in which someone is hiding assets or skimming money from the joint bank account is a sorry marriage.

In extreme situations—if a woman is being abused either physically or emotionally—she may need to squirrel away money to get out of a horrible or life-threatening relationship.

But that is the extreme.

If you had enough faith in your man to marry him and trust him with your life, you need to trust him with your money. More important, if you are going to have children with him and trust him with *their* lives, you should trust him enough to divulge everything about your finances, even assets you want to keep separate from your community property.

But trust doesn't mean turning over complete control to the degree that you are clueless about the family finances. As Ronald Reagan said when negotiating with the Soviets, "Trust, but verify."

## THAT LITTLE WHITE LIE ABOUT THAT LITTLE BLACK DRESS CAN LEAD TO A BIG FIGHT ABOUT FINANCES

Have you ever hidden a shopping bag full of clothes in the trunk of the car or in the back of the closet to keep your honey from finding out how much money you spent at the mall?

Do you intercept credit card statements so your spouse won't yell at you for overspending?

If you answered yes to one or both of these questions, you have plenty of company. In one survey of a thousand married couples conducted for *Reader's Digest,* 48 percent of wives and 49 percent of husbands said they kept how much they paid for something from their spouses.

Interestingly, couples with higher incomes lied more about what they spent.

"I don't like to tell him how much I spend when I go shopping," a wife of forty-three years told a reporter for *Reader's Digest.* "I'm afraid he'll cut back on the budget."

What is going on here? If you're lying to your husband about purchases, shame on you. And if you're lording over the family finances, making your husband feel like he's your child waiting for his weekly allowance, shame on you, too.

One way to stop the lies is to create a fair and equitable system in which each partner has his or her own pocket money. That doesn't mean setting up separate accounts. Just allocate a certain amount that you each can spend without any judgment. Consider this money your personal allowance. You can't and shouldn't be judged on how you use it.

You might ask yourself, *How harmful is it to keep quiet about what I spent on a pair of shoes or a stereo system?* You might feel entitled to spend the money you make the way you want. But keeping secrets and failing to communicate about your spending is a symptom of a big problem in your partnership. Your sneaky spending is sabotaging your family's financial goals, and lying about how much you spend is no trivial matter.

Don't just believe me; read this letter I received from a reader in Seattle: "My husband came clean to me that he borrowed $40,000 from a close friend. His rationale was that our kids were in private school, which is where I wanted them to be, and we couldn't afford it. The friend was under the impression that I knew about the loan. This has put a huge strain on our relationship. I quit my job when our third child was born. We now have five children. I have always left the money up to him because he's a CPA, and I thought he should handle it. Now it's so convoluted I can't figure it out. He's never balanced the checkbook. In the past, he has taken out credit cards without telling me. I don't want to divorce him, but it has been touch-and-go. I don't trust him as far as I can see him."

Here's one story of a husband who was leading a secret debt life:

Before I married my ex-husband, we had the money discussion. I laid out my debts (car payment, mortgage, credit cards) and my income. He told me how much he was making, but said that he had no debts besides a car payment that would be gone by the time the wedding rolled around. I believed him; marriage is about trust, right? Besides, he was still living with his parents, so it was entirely possible.

Nine months after we got married, we went Christmas shopping at the local mall. I went to the ATM to get $10 for lunch at the food court and was floored when the receipt said we only had $250 in the account, especially since we'd both gotten paid the day before. After listening to me rage at the bank for its "stupid accounting mistake," he decided to come clean that he'd had a credit card he had to make a payment on. Talk about a stunning revelation! He wouldn't tell me how much debt he had. He said it was none of my business. Since I hadn't paid all of the month's bills by then, it was the first time in my life that I had to skip payments on anything.

I found out that he'd taken out a loan before we got married and used his newly paid-off car as the collateral. I discovered this when the bank called threatening to repossess his car for nonpayment.

Talk about a stunning revelation! He didn't consider his money problems to be any business of mine, even though [they were] bringing my credit into jeopardy. When I finally filed for divorce, he told me, "I never thought you'd do this to me over money." I told him it didn't have anything to do with the money, honey.

Yet another example of why it's important to get a credit report on each other before getting married. Bad credit shouldn't necessarily sink a relationship, but it's only fair for each partner to know what he or she is getting into. Keeping secrets ruins relationships.

# 18

---

# PLAY DEFENSE
# IN THE CREDIT GAME

One of the top reasons men and women have low credit scores is credit card debt. Here's something you should understand if you have credit cards: Credit is a game, and you had better know the rules.

If you're going to use credit cards, you need to manage them to maximize your credit score. To begin, you should know that credit scores take into account the following factors:

- How long the account has been open

- Late payments

- Current balance

- Current balance compared with the credit limit

- Recent activity in the account

- How many of your credit card accounts have balances

Here are some common misconceptions about credit scoring:

• **Closed credit card accounts are deleted from your credit report:** False. Credit card account history is not immediately removed from your credit report after you close the account. It will continue to be considered by credit-scoring models. Under federal law, credit bureaus must remove negative records from your credit report after seven years. However, the bureaus may keep positive records on your report much longer.

• **Reducing your credit line will improve your credit score:** False. You may have heard that having a lot of available (unused) credit is regarded by lenders as risky, and will lower your score. This is not true for most scoring models. Available credit by itself is not considered in the FICO score, because it is not as predictive of future repayment risk as how you have managed actual debt.

• **Having a lot of unused credit accounts can hurt your score:** False. Generally speaking, the lower your balance compared with your maximum credit limit, the lower your risk of missing payments in the future and the better your credit score will be. So having credit card accounts with very low or no balances due will often improve your score.

• **Closing unused credit card accounts can boost your score:** False. Closing credit card accounts can sometimes result in a dip in your score. You should not close an account just before applying for a new loan because doing so could lower your score and hurt your chances for a good interest rate. However, you may want to close credit card accounts for other reasons. For instance, you may feel that having spare credit cards will tempt you to overspend. In addition, the fewer cards you have, the less likely it is that you might miss fraudulent charges made by some crook.

Finally, here are some tips to help you decide which accounts to close and which ones to keep:

- If you're going to close accounts, cancel retail cards before bank-issued cards. Bank cards include Visa, MasterCard, American Express, and Discover. Retail cards include department store and specialty store cards. Bank cards are tougher to qualify for, so they typically have a bigger impact on your score.

- Keep your older credit card accounts open. The longer you demonstrate that you can manage credit responsibly, the better your score will likely be. Don't close accounts you've had for a long time.

- Leave at least one credit card account open. Research shows that consumers who use credit card accounts moderately— by keeping low balances and repaying them on time—have slightly better repayment risk than consumers who do not use revolving credit at all.

Credit scores are becoming the most important financial number in people's lives. For couples, it's imperative that you understand how they work.

Credit scores reflect only your own past credit history and not your income, marital status, occupation, or other personal characteristics.

"Despite all of the news coverage about credit scores over the past year, many consumers still do not understand important facts about these increasingly influential numbers," said Stephen Brobeck, executive director of the Consumer Federation of America (CFA).

How would you answer this question: A married couple has a combined credit score—true or false?

It's false. You might be able to marry for money, but you can't marry your way into a good credit score. Debt that is jointly owed can affect your credit score as an individual. However, couples don't have a combined credit score.

To help consumers learn more about credit scoring, CFA and Fair Isaac have teamed up and produced a brochure that is distributed at no cost by the federal government's Federal Citizen Information Center. To get a copy of *Your Credit Scores,* contact the center at (888)878-3256 or write to: Credit Scores, Pueblo, CO 81009. The brochure is also available online at www.pueblo .gsa.gov. Click on the link for "Your Credit Scores Publication."

So what is it that you don't know that you should know about credit scoring? Here are some basic facts:

- FICO credit scores range from 300 to 850. A score above 700 indicates that you are a relatively low credit risk and will likely qualify for the best interest rates. Consumers with scores below 600 are typically charged higher loan rates. A low credit score can cost you not only thousands of dollars a year in additional finance charges, but potentially also insurance, telephone service, an apartment, or even a job.

- You don't have just one credit score. Each of the three major credit bureaus—Equifax, TransUnion, and Experian—generates a credit score for you. That means you could have three different credit scores, because your credit history at each bureau may be different.

- Not all lenders use all three credit scores. Some may grant you credit or approve your auto loan, for example, based on a single bureau's score, or on all three. Mortgage lenders typically consider all three of your credit scores. In the case of a home loan, lenders often use the score that falls in the middle (not an average of the three).

- The two most important factors in determining your credit score are your payment history (do you pay your bills on time?) and how much you owe.

- The fastest way to raise your credit score is to pay bills promptly and keep your credit card balances low. Want a better score? Then pay off debt rather than moving it from one credit card to another.

What I found extremely useful in *Your Credit Scores* were the hypothetical examples of how certain credit usage can change your credit scores for the better or worse over time.

In one example, a woman starts out with a credit score of 780. However, she divorces and her ex-husband agrees to make the payment on two joint credit cards. (She doesn't realize her name is still on the cards.) The ex then nearly maxes out the cards and fails to make payments on time. As a result, the woman's credit score drops 180 points to 600.

When the woman gets her former husband to roll over the balances on both cards to a new card that he opens in his name only, paying off the two accounts improves her score by 80 points in just one month.

Here's what else you can do to improve your credit score over time:

- Pay off debt rather than shifting it around to new or other credit cards. Owing the same amount of money but on fewer cards could actually lower your credit score. Let's say you owe $5,000 on three credit cards. You get an offer in the mail that would allow you to consolidate all that debt onto one card with a $5,000 credit limit at 0 percent. Wait. This may not be a good strategy. Although the interest rate is a good deal, you'll change your credit profile. Using more than 50 percent of the available balance on any credit card is not good. However, if you're not in the market for credit (a car loan or mortgage), you may want to take advantage of such an offer because you do save some money. The money you save may be a good trade-off for the hit you might take to your credit score. But let the debt linger longer than a year, and any savings could be lost if your score stays low. That results in higher interest costs in the future.

- Don't open credit card accounts that you don't need just to increase your available credit. This approach could backfire and actually lower your score.

- Get current. If you have missed payments, get current and stay current, even if that means making just the minimum payment. The longer you pay your bills on time, the better your score.

- Don't close unused credit card accounts as a short-term strategy to raise your score. A closed account will still show up on your credit report, and it may be considered in calculating your credit score.

- Don't be tempted by offers to "quick-fix" your way out of credit trouble. Don't believe any folks who say they can get rid of bad debts. No one can legally remove accurate negative information from your credit report.

- Check your credit report. If you're worried that you've damaged your credit during the holiday or the past year, check your report and credit score. This won't affect your score, as long as you order the credit report directly from the credit reporting agency or through an organization authorized to provide credit reports to consumers.

Keep this in mind: It will take time to improve your credit, but your actions going forward are just as important as the mistakes you've made in the past.

## CORRECTING CREDIT REPORTING ERRORS

I'm constantly advising people to check their credit report. But what should you do if you find an error?

First, you should know that under the Fair Credit Reporting Act, the credit bureaus and any businesses that supply them with data are supposed to correct inaccurate information in your report.

I used the word *supposed* because, in practice, getting erroneous information removed from your credit file can be like climbing Mount Everest—a cold, hard, and exasperating expedition.

That's what Judy Thomas found out. It took the Oregon real estate agent six years and a lawsuit to get TransUnion to remove the name and bad credit history of another woman from her credit file.

Thomas's lawsuit resulted in one of the largest awards ever made in such a case. A jury agreed that Thomas should receive $300,000 for the harm to her reputation and health and $5 million in punitive damages.

The judge overseeing the case recently reduced the punitive

award to $1 million while allowing the $300,000 one to stand, according to Michael C. Baxter, Thomas's Portland, Oregon–based attorney.

Baxter, who specializes in representing consumers in disputes with credit reporting agencies, said the Thomas lawsuit highlighted a major flaw in how credit bureaus investigate consumer complaints. "The bureaus go back to the source, and the creditor often just confirms the erroneous information," he said. "It's crazy.

"I have a case in which the person would have been only five years old when an account was opened," Baxter added. "It's hilarious."

It also can be maddening. "There were days when I went home in tears," Thomas said. "Creditors would say to me, 'Lady, just pay the bill.' But it wasn't my debt. The bad information would be taken off my credit report and then put back again."

Despite her ordeal, Thomas still believes it is best to try to get inaccurate information removed from your credit file. Here's what you should do, according to the Federal Trade Commission (FTC):

- Tell each credit reporting agency in writing what information you believe is inaccurate and request a deletion or correction. Provide your complete name and address. Your letter should clearly identify each item in your report that you dispute.

- Enclose a copy of your report with the items in question circled.

- Include copies (not originals) of documents that support your position.

- Send your letter by certified mail, return receipt requested, so you can prove that the credit bureau received the information.

- Keep records of everything and everyone you talk to. ("If you have to start a whole new file cabinet, do it," Thomas said.)

- You may need to send your letter to all three major bureaus if the information is incorrect in all of your credit files. These credit bureaus are Equifax (P.O. Box 740241, Atlanta, GA 30374; 800-685-1111); Experian (P.O. Box 2002, Allen, TX 75013; 888-397-3742); and TransUnion (P.O. Box 1000, Chester, PA 19022; 800-916-8800). You can also dispute information online with all three companies, at www.equifax.com, www.experian.com, and www.tuc.com. You will need a current copy of your credit report.

Here's what is supposed to happen after you've made your case:

- The law requires credit agencies to investigate disputed information and correct inaccuracies within thirty days of hearing from a consumer.

- The credit bureaus must forward all relevant data you provide about the dispute to the information provider. But I wouldn't wait for that to happen. Call and then send your own letter with copies of all documents supporting your position to whatever business or creditor is supplying the wrong data to the credit bureau.

- When both the information provider and credit bureau investigations are complete, you must be given written results and a free copy of your report if the dispute results in a change.

- A reinvestigation may not resolve your dispute. If that happens, ask the credit agency to include your statement of the dispute in your file and in future reports.

If you don't get satisfactory action from the credit bureau, you have at least two recourses. You can complain to the FTC. To file a complaint, go to www.ftc.gov, call (877)382-4357, or write to the Consumer Response Center, CRC-240, Federal Trade Commission, Washington, DC 20580.

Unfortunately, the FTC does not resolve individual consumer problems. Nonetheless, your complaint might lead to some law enforcement action.

Your second option is to file a lawsuit. "The more people who file lawsuits, the more the consumer reporting agencies will have to change their methods," Thomas said.

Baxter warned, however, that this type of case is hard to win and is costly for the consumer. Still, if you have a particularly egregious case, go for it. You may find a lawyer to take the case on contingency, meaning he or she would get paid only if you win an award. The American Bar Association has a web page (www .abanet.org/legalservices/lris/directory.html) with links to state lawyer referral programs.

If you want to catch errors early, get a copy of your credit report at least once a year. Check it thoroughly, and immediately dispute any inaccuracies.


## WHAT'S THE SCORE?*

FICO scores are calculated from a lot of different credit data in your credit report. This data can be grouped into five categories, as outlined below. The percentages in the chart reflect how important each of the categories is in determining your score.

*This section through page 150 is reprinted courtesy of the Fair Isaac Corp.

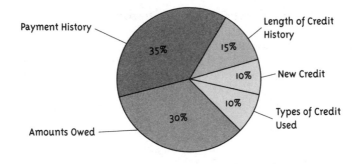

### *Payment history*

- Account payment information on specific types of accounts (credit cards, retail accounts, installment loans, finance company accounts, mortgage, et cetera).

- Presence of adverse public records (bankruptcy, judgments, lawsuits, liens, wage attachments, et cetera), collection items, and/or delinquency (past due items).

- Severity of delinquency.

- Amount past due on delinquent accounts or collection items.

- Time since past due items, adverse public records (if any), or collection items (if any).

- Number of past due items on file.

- Number of accounts paid as agreed.

### *Amounts owed*

- Amount owing on accounts.

- Amount owing on specific types of accounts.

- Lack of a specific type of balance, in some cases.

- Number of accounts with balances.

- Proportion of credit lines used.

- Proportion of balance to original loan amount (on certain types of installment loans).

### *Length of credit history*

- Time since accounts opened.

- Time since accounts opened, by specific type of account.

- Time since account activity.

### *New credit*

- Number of recently opened accounts, and proportion of accounts that were recently opened, by type of account.

- Number of recent credit inquiries.

- Time since recent account opening(s), by type of account.

- Time since credit inquiry(s).

- Reestablishment of positive credit history following past payment problems.

### *Types of credit used*

- Number of (presence, prevalence, and recent information on) various types of accounts (credit cards, retail accounts, installment loans, mortgage, consumer finance accounts, et cetera).

## OUTDATED CREDIT ADVICE

Married women are continually told that they need to keep a credit card in their own name to maintain a credit history. If they don't, they are warned, they could have trouble getting credit after a divorce.

Such advice is outdated. If a husband and wife have joint credit card accounts, information about those accounts appears on both people's credit files. As a result, both their credit scores will benefit (or suffer) from how that joint credit card is handled. The credit-scoring models don't distinguish between an account held individually and one held jointly. The scoring models don't know when people divorce.

If you have a good credit score when you divorce, then you should have little trouble qualifying for a new credit card account after a divorce.

The bottom line: The credit report and credit score of a person isn't affected per se by a marriage or divorce, because a couple never has a rating as a couple.

## DEBT HAPPENS

Debt happens to the best of us. You lose a job. You get divorced. You overspend. In fact, most adults—67 percent of women, 74 percent of men—enter marriage with at least some debt. Of those with debt, about half owe more than $5,000, primarily from auto loans, credit cards, student loans, and medical bills, research associate David Schramm of Utah State University found in a study of 1,010 newlyweds.

Consumer debt is at an all-time high. Consider these facts:

- The average household credit card debt is $9,200, according to CardWeb.com.

- Research by the Federal Reserve indicates that household debt is at a record high relative to disposable income.

- Consumer bankruptcies remain at historic highs, well above the 1.5 million record first set in 2002. There were close to 1.6 million personal bankruptcy petitions filed in 2004. And, according to bankruptcy researchers Elizabeth Warren and Amelia Warren Tyagi, authors of *The Two-Income Trap,* for every family that officially declares bankruptcy, there are seven more whose debt loads suggest they ought to.

- Each year, almost nine million consumers seek help from debt counseling services.

- The average client seeking help from a consumer credit counseling agency has $30,000 in gross income and more than $15,700 in unsecured consumer debt.

Take a moment to reflect on this last fact. Some people are carrying consumer debt (mostly from credit cards) that is just a little more than half their gross pay. Not net, but gross.

Whatever the cause of your debt, don't beat yourself up. Maybe it will help you feel better to know that you are not alone. In one online survey of five thousand people, conducted by Consolidated Credit Counseling Services—a nonprofit organization that helps people with debt and money management issues—63 percent of those interviewed said debts were making their home life unhappy, and 43 percent had a debt-to-income ratio of 50 percent or more. Here are Consolidated's other findings:

$ 58 percent had credit cards at or near their maximum credit limit.

$ 62 percent did not have a savings account.

$ 92 percent did not have a three-month emergency fund.

$ 37 percent took cash advances from one credit card to make payments on another credit card.

$ 59 percent paid only the minimum amount due on credit cards each month.

So if you fit into one of the categories, how do you fix a debt problem?

First and foremost, put your credit cards away. You can't get out of debt while you're still using debt.

> **"Think what you do when you run into debt; you give to another power over your liberty."**
>
> **Benjamin Franklin**

Here are some other ways to reduce your debt:

• **Face the truth:** Before you can reduce your debt, you need to be honest about how much you actually have. So gather all your credit card statements and any other outstanding bills (opened and unopened) and total them up. Once you see that bottom-line number, perhaps that will be the wake-up call you need to realize that your debt is crunching you.

• **Create a plan:** If you are not going to seek help from a credit counseling agency, then you need to develop a systematic way to pay down your debts. List your debts, starting with the ones charging you the most interest. Those are the debts you want to tackle first. Direct the majority of your payments toward paying off these bills. If you can, pay something on all your bills, but any extra money should go to reduce the debt carrying the highest interest rate.

• **Sweat the small stuff:** If you have a lot of small debts—less than $300—pay them off in full even if it means skipping a payment or making just the minimum payment on another bill. Paying off the small stuff first will do two things. You won't have a lot of small creditors reporting your delinquency to the credit bureaus. Being late on small debts dings your credit score the same as being late on large ones. Getting rid of these smaller bills will also give you a feeling of accomplishment.

• **Keep saving:** Readers will often ask me if they should stop saving while they are paying down their debts. Absolutely not. Even if you can only save $5 out of every paycheck, do it. The reason people continue to pile on more debt while they are trying to get out of debt is that they have no financial cushion. Whenever something happens (and it always does), they are forced to use their credit cards because they have no savings.

• **Understand the difference between good and bad debt:** Bad debt is using credit to buy anything that you can eat, drink, or wear. Good debt is money borrowed to buy or pay for something that has the potential to appreciate. Borrowing to buy a home is good debt. Borrowing to pay for a college education is good debt. Your goal should be to limit the amount of debt you use to accumulate assets that depreciate the moment you leave the store or car lot. Therefore, paying off bad debt should be your top priority. Remember, when you use your credit card, you are getting a loan. Each time you reach for your credit card, ask yourself if you would go into a bank branch and ask for a loan for whatever it is that you're about to buy.

---

**"A good debt is not as good as no debt."**

**Chinese proverb**

---

• **Pay as you go:** If you can't pay off your credit card bill every month, you're in debt trouble. Before charging anything, ask yourself if you can pay it off by the due date. If not, don't say "Charge it."

> **"Our business is to have great credit and to use it little."**
> **Thomas Jefferson**

• **Just say no:** You won't get rid of your debt if you're still in a buy mode. This means you have to stop buying anything that is not absolutely necessary. Every time you go shopping, ask this question: *Is this a need or is this a want?* If you are in a debt crisis, every single spare penny ought to be used to reduce your debt load. You need to eliminate, not accumulate more stuff.

• **Pay off debt** rather than shifting it around to new or other credit cards.

• **Clean house:** If you want the best incentive to stop spending, clean your house. Go through every closet and cabinet and set out any items you haven't used in two years. Whenever I do this, it immediately kills any urge to splurge. I realize that I already have too much stuff.

Perhaps neither you nor your husband is in debt trouble—or so you think. You both pay off your credit cards every month. Don't be smug if that is the case. You may still be overspending. A controlled study conducted at the Sloan School of Management at MIT by two professors, Drazen Prelec and Duncan Simester, found that when people pay with a credit card, they are more likely to pay more for what they are buying—as much as 100 percent more.

The study also demonstrated that consumers spend more when they use credit rather than cash. The researchers called this financial phenomenon the "credit card premium."

## CREDIT COUNSELING

**"No man's credit is ever as good as his money."**
                                            **Edgar Watson Howe**

Many credit counseling agencies may be classified as nonprofit, but they aren't in business for the public good. They are often connected to profit-making ventures, such as companies that make debt-consolidation loans.

In fact, so many of these operations are questionable that the Internal Revenue Service, the Federal Trade Commission, and an array of state regulators recently teamed up to warn people about the problems that can occur when using an unscrupulous credit counseling organization. Some debtors, for example, end up paying high fees to set up a debt-repayment plan. Others end up with worse credit records than they had before they sought help because the credit counseling agencies don't pay their clients' bills on time—or at all.

You should know that credit counseling agencies are, in essence, debt-collection middlemen. They negotiate with creditors on a debtor's behalf to, among other things, reduce the interest rate on a credit card and sometimes waive or reduce late fees and penalties. In return, debtors make one monthly payment to the credit counseling agency, which then forwards the money to creditors.

In the past, credit counseling agencies rarely charged for their services because they were paid by creditors, who saw the debt plans as a chance to recoup what they were owed. But so many consumers have signed up for debt-repayment plans these days that creditors are less motivated to cut debtors any slack. Many of the ads promising a huge reduction in the interest rate you pay are just not true.

If you sign up for a debt plan, expect to be charged a setup fee and a monthly fee. Some agencies charge as much as a full month's consolidated payment—usually hundreds of dollars—simply to establish an account. Before signing up with a credit agency, follow these tips:

• **Watch out for high fees:** In general, if the setup fee for a debt-management plan is more than $50 and the monthly fee more than $25, look for a better deal. However, if the agency is offering extra services such as budget counseling or an educational program, it's reasonable for them to charge extra. Still, you don't have to spend hundreds of dollars to find a good credit counseling agency.

• **Watch out for unreasonable promises:** Creditors, not agencies, determine which concessions may be made. Any agency that claims it can *guarantee* a reduction in your payments or interest rate is misleading you. Many creditors are becoming increasingly unwilling to reduce interest rates for consumers who enter debt-management programs. Several major credit card issuers increase the interest rate for consumers using debt-repayment plans.

• **Understand what services are being offered:** If you are promised anything, get it in writing. Watch out for outrageous claims. One credit counseling organization I found on the Internet promises people they can pay off their credit card debt for 50 cents on the dollar. For instance, if your debt is $2,000, the company claims it can get you a deal in which you only have to pay $1,000. Credit card companies rarely, if ever, settle for less money than owed.

• **Watch out for high monthly service charges:** Most agencies now charge monthly fees for debt-management programs, also known as debt-consolidation plans. There are enough good agencies with low fees that you shouldn't pay an amount you can't afford. If the agency is vague or reluctant to talk about specific fees, walk away.

• **Seek real counseling:** Any agency that offers you a debt-management plan in less than twenty minutes hasn't spent enough time looking at your finances. Keep in mind that even if the agency is a nonprofit, it is not necessarily a benevolent organization. An effective counseling session, whether on the phone or in person, takes significant time.

• **An agency cannot remove negative information from your credit report if it's true:** It is illegal for any organization to represent that negative information, such as a judgment or bankruptcy, can be removed from your credit report. Most negative information remains on your credit report for seven years. A bankruptcy stays on for ten years.

• **Check whether your creditors are actually receiving their money:** Missed payments by the credit counseling agency will still be reported to the credit bureaus.

• **Do some homework:** Call your local Better Business Bureau to find out whether the credit counseling organization you're thinking about using has a history of problems with clients. Go to the website for the National Association of State Charities Officials (www.nasconet.org) and find the state agency that has oversight of charitable groups in your area. Check to see whether any complaints have been filed against the nonprofit.

If you are having financial trouble because of poor money management, remember, a debt-repayment plan is just a temporary solution to a long-term problem. If you do have to use a credit counseling company, find one that offers some real counseling. Debt consolidation should be a once-in-a-lifetime experience.

# 19

## A TAXING TIME

Each year, thousands of women find themselves liable for tax debts incurred by their husbands. Here's a typical case. A reader wrote: "A friend of mine got married and was looking forward to getting her tax refund, as she always did, and found that her new husband had unpaid debts to both the state and the Feds. Her refund went to pay his debts."

In far too many households, wives are letting their husbands do the taxes. The wife simply signs the form presented to her. That may be okay if your man is honest and your marriage is strong. But what if he turns out to be a lying dog?

Congress has finally recognized this problem. As a result of changes in the tax code, divorcing or legally separated spouses can choose to be held accountable only for taxes on their own income.

Under the "innocent spouse exception," a spouse may not have to pay the tax, interest, and penalties on a joint return if she or he had no reason to know that there was a substantial understatement of the taxes. But this is very difficult to prove in court, and it can be a costly exercise.

You are considered an innocent spouse if you "did not know, and had no reason to know" that your partner was a tax scofflaw. Still, how do you prove a negative? How do you prove you did not know?

Even if you are keeping records that might help prove you didn't know your spouse was a cheat, it seems to me that the fact that you're keeping records suggests you must have suspected something. Besides, the IRS takes a dim view of people living large, then claiming they don't know the details of the family finances.

On the other hand, women who are truly innocent but are not keeping track of things often have only their word that they didn't know what their scoundrel of a husband was up to. (The husband is almost always the bum, though a woman might be the guilty party on rare occasions.)

A wife ought to be able to trust her husband. And many do. I did.

Even though I have a master's degree in business and write about financial issues for a living, I would rather eat nails than fill out those confusing tax forms and figure out what deductions I'm entitled to. I start getting headaches in January anticipating that darn April 15 deadline.

I was more than happy to leave the preparation of our joint tax return to my husband, who began doing my individual tax return years before we got married. (I was too cheap to use an accountant.) On occasion, I even had the audacity to protest his constant barrage of questions. "I don't have time for this," I would say. "Can't you just do my taxes and leave me alone?"

And, I'll confess, I never really reviewed the information once he filled the forms out. I simply asked him where I should sign.

My behavior was, to put it bluntly, just plain stupid. Unfortunately, according to tax experts, it's all too common.

There are a lot of spouses who just don't pay attention. Often one spouse takes responsibility for the family finances, including the tax process. But not being aware can come back to haunt you.

It's typical for one spouse to ignore the tax preparation process and sign off without understanding what's on the tax forms.

One Virginia woman who wrote to me said that during her thirteen years of marriage, she never reviewed the tax forms her husband prepared. In fact, she said that her husband—whom she later divorced—would use his hands to block her view of salary information or make her sign a blank tax form.

"I was so naive and so dumb," she said. "I never knew how much he made. I just thought that was the way it was. I had so much confidence in him that I just didn't care. I didn't worry about the taxes."

Nothing could be more important than being involved in filing your taxes and understanding as best you can what's included in your filing. And remember: If you are married and filing jointly, you and your spouse are equally responsible for everything on that tax form—even if you didn't help prepare it.

It's critical that you help in the preparation of your joint taxes. At the very least, review the forms. Keep this in mind: You may be held responsible for all the tax due, even if your spouse earned all the income or claimed improper deductions or credits. There are some situations in which you can get "innocent spouse relief" from this joint and individual liability, but the hurdles are high.

I now review our taxes. I ask questions, and my husband and I use tax time to revise our family budget. It wasn't easy for me to change my ways—and I still hate tax time. But I make the time, and so should you.

## INNOCENT SPOUSE

In order to qualify for spousal relief, you must meet certain conditions. For more information on whether you qualify, go to www.irs.gov. In the search field, type in "innocent spouse." You can also download IRS Publication 971, *Innocent Spouse Relief.*

To qualify for innocent spouse relief, you must meet all of the following conditions:

- You must have filed a joint return that has an understatement of tax.

- The understatement of tax must be due to errors by your spouse.

- You must establish that at the time you signed the joint return, you did not know, and had no reason to know, that there was an understatement of tax.

- Taking into account all of the facts and circumstances, you must show it would be unfair to hold you liable for the understatement of tax.

- You must request relief within two years after the date on which the IRS first began collection activity against you after July 22, 1998.

## WHEN THE TAX MAN COMETH

When April 15 draws near, take off the blinders, push your fears to the side, and become involved in helping your spouse prepare your tax return. Here's what you can do:

- As the mail carrier brings your tax information, such as your W-2 forms, start looking it over. Don't wait for everything to pile up, when it can seem too daunting. Take this time to review your investment information and other financial documents.

- If an accountant or a tax-filing service is preparing your return, be sure that both you and your spouse go to the appointment. It's important that you both be present to discuss the preparation of your taxes. You should know—and you have a right to know—what is on the tax return.

- When reviewing your tax filing, if you don't understand something, ask about it. Carefully look over the various schedules, which can detail such things as the ownership of rental property and various investments. Such information can become especially important in the event of a death or divorce.

- Don't sigh and sign. Your signature on those tax forms makes you responsible for the information supplied to the IRS.

- Don't let your spouse or anyone else persuade you to sign a blank tax form. Never sign your tax return without first looking over the statement.

- Use tax time as a chance to do some financial planning. Take a look at how you are spending your money and what investments you have. Think of it as a once-a-year checkup—a sort of annual physical for your finances.

## 20

---

# SURVIVAL SKILLS
# ON ONE SALARY

How does a family live on one paycheck when two don't seem to stretch far enough? I found myself asking that question while contemplating a Census Bureau report noting that more women are leaving the workforce to stay home and care for their infants. In 2003, the United States had an estimated 5.5 million stay-at-home parents—5.4 million moms and 98,000 dads.

A 2003 opinion poll conducted by SurveyUSA showed that a staggering 87 percent of U.S. moms with children age twelve and under said they would prefer to be home if they could afford to.

If you're contemplating leaving the outside workforce to become a stay-at-home mom, sit down with your husband and really crunch the numbers to see if it can work for your family financially. The decision to stay at home is going to take a lot of financial planning and determination to get rid of expenses that you may once have considered necessities.

Overall, most mothers do return to work before their baby is a year old. Those who don't are most likely to be white women, thirty years or older, with one or more years of college and husbands who presumably have good jobs. Even if you don't fit that profile, there's a chance you may be able to afford to stay home. Here's how:

• **Tally your take-home pay:** Do the math. You may realize you can afford to quit your job without significantly changing your lifestyle. To see what it costs you to work, go to http://www .inforeferral.com/calculators/calculator20.htm for a real hourly wage calculator. You may realize that by the time you pay taxes on your income, child care expenses, transportation, and so forth, your net pay isn't that much.

• **Cut your expenses:** Right now I bet you're thinking, *Please— we're living paycheck to paycheck.* Once you stop working, however, many of your work-related expenses (clothes for work, commuting costs, eating lunch out) will go down. When you add up all the little expenses, you'll be surprised at how much you can save.

• **Don't try to do it all:** You may not be able to save enough to meet all of your financial goals, such as funding your retirement and footing the entire bill for your child's college education. If you have to choose, save for retirement first. Suppose you're a thirty-year-old parent who began saving for retirement the year your child was born. Assume you retire at sixty-seven and had a starting salary of $35,000, which increased 3 percent each year until retirement. You could have more than $750,000 if you invested about 6 percent of your salary in a 401(k) and received a 3 percent employer match with an annual return of 7 percent. Conversely, a person who began saving for retirement after sending a child to college would have just over $185,000 at retirement. Your child can borrow to go to college; you can't borrow to pay for your retirement.

• **Stand by your man:** It sounds a little corny, but if someone is going to stay at home, it's going to take a team effort.

For many mothers, staying at home isn't an option. According to the Census Bureau, the number of mothers leaving the workforce to stay at home with their infants did not decline among women under age thirty, African Americans, Hispanics, and those who had a high school education or less.

These women work because if they don't, their families will suffer. In other cases, parents work to support not just their children but a host of less fortunate relatives. And still other families see a two-income household as their ticket to a better life—one without financial struggle.

Ultimately, you have to do what you think is right for your family. But if you have the choice to stay at home, planning and some sacrifice can help you trade in your long commute and a boss who gets on your nerves for more time with your children.

## STAY-AT-HOME PARENTING REQUIRES FINANCIAL FORETHOUGHT

"The one thing I regret is that we didn't save more," said one stay-at-home mother. "And I would have made sure we paid off all our credit cards so we could be a lot more comfortable."

It's not that she and her husband didn't plan to have a family. They just hadn't given much thought to whether one of them would stay at home to raise their children. "I always thought I would work," said the mom, who worked for an economic consulting firm. "At the spur of the moment I just decided I wanted to quit. There was no planning involved."

Even so, the couple made some decisions that have allowed

them to live off one income. For example, unlike many well-paid professionals, they bought a modest, Tudor-style home instead of a megamansion with all the modern trimmings—the Jacuzzi bathtub, walk-in closets, and huge family room. It wasn't that they bought down; they just didn't feel the need to keep up with the Joneses.

> **"Never keep up with the Joneses. Drag them down to your level. It's cheaper."**
>
> **Quentin Crisp**

"We didn't want to be strapped down to a mortgage we couldn't handle," said the stay-at-home mom, whose husband is a doctor. That decision gave them much more flexibility in their budget and allowed them to send their daughter to a private school.

As more couples move up the ladder, the decision for Mom or Dad to stay at home becomes a real option. But poor financial planning and overspending can quickly take away that choice.

In fact, engaged couples should be talking about whether one of them might want to stay home with the baby. To make living on one income work, you have to do some preplanning—and when you do, you may find that you don't want to commit to an expensive car or house if either spouse may want to stay at home one day.

It's hard to go down to one income if your lifestyle is stuffed with expenses that require two salaries. From the very beginning of your marriage, you ought to include in your financial planning the possibility that one of you might stay at home. With that in mind, every financial decision should include this question: *Could we afford that on one salary?* Every choice, from what car you buy to which home to purchase, should be predicated on the assumption that one spouse might want to stay home.

Often couples' options are limited because they are mired in debt or have overextended themselves financially—even while bringing home salaries that top six figures. Certainly, having a baby doesn't automatically make you a better money manager. Bad spending habits are hard to break and even harder to manage on one salary.

Even though her husband is a doctor, our stay at-home-mom said she had to train herself to be a more frugal person. "During my working days, I lived in Saks and Nordstrom. Now I shop at Nordstrom Rack," she noted. She joked that at any given time her husband isn't sure which long-distance carrier they are using because she switches whenever one makes a better offer. She clips coupons and takes her daughter's clothes to a consignment shop.

None of these money-saving strategies occurred to her before she decided to stay at home, but things would be easier now if she had done some planning.

As you're planning your family, take some financial steps to prepare for life on just one income. Here are some things to think about:

- The long term. Early on, before you decide to have a baby, include in your financial planning the possibility that either Mom or Dad might stay home.

- Try to avoid living it up before baby comes. It's easy when you have two incomes and no children to charge up those credit cards. But keep your debts down. Pay off your credit cards before the baby comes. And save as much as you can— to help prepare for when there is just one income.

- Haven't bought a house yet? Think modestly, which will give you the option of staying at home. Consider buying a home you could afford on one income. Remember, the baby may come before you have a chance to trade up to a better home, so ask yourself, *Can we live comfortably in this house with our children?*

- Keep up your professional skills. Don't drop your office contacts. Eventually you may want to return to work, and the transition will be easier if you maintain your skills—by taking continuing education classes, for instance.

- Retirement. Used to be, nonworking spouses could contribute only $250 to an individual retirement account (the IRS calls it an "individual retirement arrangement"). But Congress finally saw the inequity in that. After all, nonworking spouses need to save for retirement, too. Now nonemployed spouses with no income can have a spousal IRA as long as the couple files a joint return and the working spouse has enough earned income to cover the contribution. In 2005–2007, you will be able to contribute $4,000 each. In 2008, you will be able to contribute up to $5,000 each. Just remember, the *I* in *IRA* stands for "individual." There is no such thing as a "joint" IRA account.

- Life insurance. If money is tight, you might be inclined to forgo getting life insurance for yourself. But that would be a mistake. Just think how much it would cost to replace your services. Actually you don't have to think. A research analysis completed by Salary.com reveals that today's 5.4 million stay-at-home moms would earn $131,471 in annual salary, including overtime pay, if paid in cash.

# PART 2: THEN COMES MARRIAGE

### *What's the Bottom Line?*

Here's what you should have learned from part 2:

✓ How much debt is okay when paying for a wedding? None! Weddings should be a cash affair—as in, all expenses should be paid with cash. If you use a credit card, make sure you pay the bill off in full. A wedding is a luxury, not a necessity. It's foolish to fund a wedding on a credit card.

✓ Fast-forward ten years. What will you remember from your wedding? If money is tight, spend what money you have on things that will have "memory value," such as the wedding photos. Trust me, if you're still married in ten years, your wedding guests won't even remember what type of flowers you had on the reception table or the wedding favor.

✓ Asking directly or indirectly for wedding guests to give you money to help pay for a car, home, maid service, or honeymoon is just being avaricious.

✓ Keeping a joint account is not that hard. Deep down, couples who object to joint accounts really are objecting to the notion that they might actually have to communicate with their spouse about what they are spending or saving (or not saving).

✓ When you get married, treat your marriage like a financial partnership. There should be no hers or his—just ours.

✓ While it's important to trust your spouse, that doesn't mean you shouldn't keep tabs on what's going on.

✓ The reward for having joint accounts is that you can rejoice in each other's financial accomplishments, because they become your own.

✓ If you want financial peace in your household, develop a set of House Rules to govern your financial behavior as a married couple.

✓ When you get married, it's not all about your wants anymore. You have another person's feelings and desires to consider. Marriage means compromising. And when you compromise, it doesn't mean there are two losers.

✓ You've got to plan so you know where you are going, and that means creating a budget.

✓ If you had enough faith in your man to marry him and trust him with your life, you need to trust him with your money.

✔ Credit is a game, and you had better know the rules. If you're going to use credit cards, you need to manage them to maximize your credit score.

✔ It's essential that you help prepare your joint tax return. Don't sign any forms until you review them thoroughly.

✔ Remember, on a joint return both taxpayers are jointly and individually responsible for the tax and any interest or penalty due on the return, even if you later divorce. If your divorce decree states that your ex is responsible for any amounts due on previously filed joint returns, you may still be held responsible for all the tax due. If your spouse did do something improper, you can apply for innocent spouse relief, but it's not easy to get.

✔ Before you decide to have a baby, include in your financial planning the possibility that either you or your spouse may want to be a stay-at-home parent.

✔ It is possible to live on one salary but it will take financial discipline. Before the baby comes, keep your debts down. If you can, buy a home that you can afford on one salary.

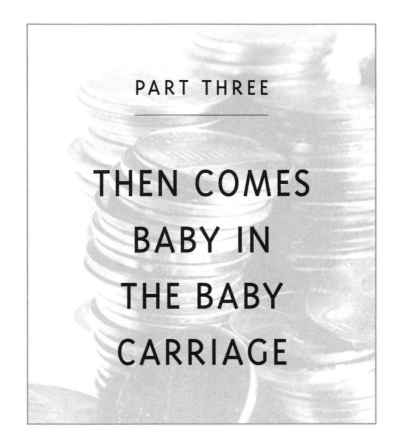

PART THREE

# THEN COMES BABY IN THE BABY CARRIAGE

# 21

---

# CREATE A FINANCIAL FOUNDATION FOR BABY

A friend of mine was more than a little annoyed at the gifts that had been suggested for a baby shower she was going to attend. "Look at this," she told me, handing me the gift registry list. "Most of this stuff costs more than $100. Please! They need to register for diapers, baby wipes, or onesies [you know, the little T-shirts with snaps]. That's what new babies really need."

I nodded in agreement during her entire tirade. I've been invited to many baby showers and, as has become the custom, I am often directed to a particular store at which I am asked to buy something from a list of gifts selected by the mother-to-be.

But rarely have I ever bought anything from the list, which far too often includes expensive baby monitors, diaper bags, strollers, and other overpriced or unnecessary baby items people probably wouldn't (or shouldn't) buy with their own money.

After three children, you can take it from me—babies don't need half the stuff you think you need. You don't need a special hooded towel to dry your baby after his or her bath—just use the towels you've got. Forget about some fancy bottle warmer. Just run hot water over the bottle.

I feel for new parents, many of whom don't always consider the costs of having a baby. According to the U.S. Department of Agriculture, families earning less than $40,700 a year spent an estimated $6,820 per year, in 2003 dollars, caring for a child from birth up to age two, including food, clothing, child care, and miscellaneous expenses. Families with incomes from $40,700 to $68,400 spent $9,510 per year, and those earning more than $68,400 spent $14,000 for the same period.

Parents need to spend less time in the baby store and more time attending to some important financial decisions when baby makes three (or four, or five). If you're expecting a baby, you need to create a financial foundation for your new addition. Here's what you should do if you're a new parent:

- Get life insurance. There is now an extra person relying on your income. It's vital that you obtain enough life insurance to help support your child if something happens to you. If you're not sure how much you need, try the life insurance needs calculator created by the Life and Health Insurance Foundation for Education at www.life-line.org. Ideally, you want enough coverage so your beneficiaries could invest the death benefit and live off any interest earned.

- Update important documents. Make sure you add the baby to any existing insurance policies and review and update other important papers, such as beneficiary information.

- If you can afford it, purchase disability insurance. If your employer offers disability insurance coverage, get enough to replace 60 to 70 percent of your income. You also need to be mindful that if your disability insurance premiums are paid entirely by your employer or with your pretax dollars, the payout, should you need it, would be taxable income. That means you could end up with a lot less money for paying monthly bills than you expected. Therefore, you may need to buy a supplemental disability insurance policy to make up the difference. When you pay for the coverage yourself with after-tax dollars, the benefit is not taxed.

- Do some estate planning. Make a will or update the one you have after the baby is born. Determine who will serve as your child's guardian if the need should arise. Depending on your situation, you may want to consider setting up a trust to ensure that your property is given to your child according to your wishes.

- Don't procrastinate. Create a college fund for your child. I don't have to tell you that the cost of a college education is expensive. So instead of spending eighteen years buying stuff he or she doesn't need or won't even remember, save as much as you can for an investment that will pay off. Over a work-life, individuals who have a Bachelor's degree would earn an average $2.1 million—about one third more than workers who did not finish college, and nearly twice as much as workers with only a high school diploma, according to the Census Bureau.

- If you fail to adequately save for your retirement, your child (and his or her spouse, most likely) may pass out when you announce that you have to move in because you don't have enough money.

## SAVING FOR COLLEGE

Many parents still aren't aware of one tax-advantaged, state-sponsored way of saving for a child's college years. In a recent survey conducted for Charles Schwab and Ariel Mutual Funds, high-income investors were asked what a 529 plan is used for. Some thought it was a way to save for retirement. It's not. It turns out 80 percent of the investors interviewed weren't sure what a 529 plan, which was named for a section of the Internal Revenue Code, is for.

Actually, there are two types of 529: a college savings plan and a prepaid tuition plan. Investing in a college savings plan is like investing in a mutual fund. Your money is combined with money from others and invested by the plan manager. The alternative, the prepaid plan, lets parents, grandparents, and other interested parties lock in today's tuition rates and then pays out future college tuition to any of a state's eligible colleges or universities (or an equal payment to private and out-of-state institutions).

There are numerous websites that will give you a good tutorial on these plans. One of the most useful is www.savingforcollege.com. This site provides a comprehensive look at all available 529 plans. Look for the link to the site's 529 evaluator. You might also try www.collegesavings.org, which is run by the College Savings Plans Network, an affiliate of the National Association of State Treasurers. Here are some of the basics of investing in a 529 plan:

- You can invest in installments or in a lump sum.

- Unlike education IRAs, 529 savings plans exclude no one from contributing on the basis of high income.

- At this point (the tax law could change after 2010), earnings are not federally taxed as long as the money is used for qualified educational expenses. Graduate, professional, and technical school expenses qualify.

- You can open an account for any child—yours, a relative's, or someone else's.

- The money in any state plan can be used at any accredited college or university, including seven hundred international schools. By the time this book is published, all fifty states and the District of Columbia will have operational college savings plans, and twenty states will also offer prepaid tuition plans to their residents, according to the College Savings Plans Network.

- Most states allow nonresidents to open an account. Many states offer their own residents a tax deduction for contributions made to their state-sponsored 529 plan. Mississippi is particularly generous with its deduction. Residents can deduct up to $10,000 per year ($20,000 for married couples filing jointly). Rhode Island is one of the stingiest, with a $500 deduction ($1,000 for a couple). In Maryland it is $2,500 per account, and in Virginia it is $2,000.

College savings plans are treated as an asset of the account holder, not the student. Prepaid tuition plans are treated as a resource, meaning that they reduce financial aid packages dollar for dollar, but only when money from the plans is actually used, and only for the amount used.

Whatever you decide to do, the sooner you start, the better your chances will be of having money to cover college expenses. The best gift for your baby is for you to plan for his or her financial future.

# 22

---

# HAVE TWO WILLS
# SO THERE'S A WAY

According to one survey, 73.6 percent of parents with one or more minor children lacked a last will and testament. Another survey, by the legal website FindLaw.com, found that 57 percent of Americans do not have a will. Nolo.com, also an online legal resource, says 70 percent of the people in the United States don't have a will.

Actually, none of the surveys are exactly right.

In a manner of speaking, we all have a will. It's just not one that we've written.

Every state dictates how a deceased person's assets will be handled. If you die intestate, as dying without a valid will is called, your assets could be distributed to a relative you can't stand or given to a trifling adult child who never had a dollar he didn't want to spend.

And what if you're on your second marriage?

Here's a scenario that has happened many times. You get married for a second time. You die. You haven't left a will. All your assets go to your new spouse. But then he dies. Now all your assets, and those of your second husband, go to his children from a previous marriage. Because you haven't made provisions for your children from your first marriage, they get nothing.

"I've done estate planning for twenty years, and I've seen what happens when people fail to plan their estates," said James Kosakow, a lawyer in Westport, Connecticut. "It's often after a parent dies that you see all the mistakes that were made, and all of a sudden people realize how important a will is."

For a basic primer on what you should have in your will, go to www.lifeadvice.com. It's a site run by MetLife that offers some practical and easy-to-understand advice on writing a will. MetLife has also created two brochures for will writing: *Planning Your Estate* and *Making a Will.* Here's what MetLife says should be part of your will:

- A description of your assets.

- The names of your spouse, children, and other beneficiaries.

- The names of alternate beneficiaries, in the event a beneficiary dies before you do.

- Specific gifts, such as a car or furniture, you want to leave to someone.

- The name of a guardian for your minor children. Also, remember to name an alternative guardian, in the event your first choice is unable or unwilling to care for the children.

- An executor who will manage the estate, including paying debts and taxes and distributing what's left over as specified in your will.

- A living trust, if you want to avoid the cost and headache of probate court, which determines according to state law how someone's assets will be disbursed.

With a living trust, your assets pass directly to your beneficiaries after you die. A living trust isn't appropriate for everyone and isn't cheap. Depending on where you live, it could cost you $1,000 to $2,000 to set one up—more if you have a large and complicated estate. If you set up a trust, you will need to name a trustee (and a backup trustee) to oversee the terms of the trust.

In addition to your will, you should have a living will. This document, which may also be called a health care directive or advance directive, spells out what kind of medical treatment you want should you become too ill to speak for yourself. For example, it will state whether you want life-prolonging procedures. You will also need to get a medical power of attorney, which allows someone you name to make decisions about your medical care.

If you want people to know how to care for you if you become incapacitated, get a living will.

If you care about leaving your family in peace after you've been put to rest, get a will.

# 23

---

# MAKING KIDS
# MONEY-WISE

When then–Treasury Secretary Paul H. O'Neill announced that his department would aggressively promote financial literacy in our schools, he said: "As we shape our children into adults, we must acknowledge that part of being an adult is to develop and understand individual financial objectives. The best place to start is in our schools, and the most effective approach is through the integration of financial education into the core curricula of reading and math."

I agree that efforts to improve personal finance programs in the schools are necessary and long overdue. But I disagree with the secretary's contention that financial literacy begins in the classroom.

The best time to start teaching your children about money is when they are young. It begins in the home with parents and other influential people in their lives.

Make no mistake about it, children learn what they live. Studies by the American Savings Education Council and the Employee Benefit Research Institute find year after year that parents underestimate the role they can play in educating their children about money. The surveys always find that students said they turn to their parents for financial education and guidance.

Yet when asked to describe what they have specifically done to teach their children about financial matters, 56 percent of parents in a survey could name only one example, 31 percent cited just two examples, and 8 percent said "nothing" or "don't know."

Whether you realize it or not, you are teaching your children about money every day, for better or worse.

Even I would never have imagined that my oldest child, Olivia, would get a lesson about saving and spending while fighting for her life.

In the summer of 2002, Olivia was diagnosed with a rare and grave condition that put her in the hospital for more than two months. During her hospital stay, she had to take an incredible amount of medication—pills that could choke a horse, liquids that made her gag, shots that turned her thighs black-and-blue. It was an awful regimen that would make Olivia collapse in tears at the sight of the nurse coming through the door. Sometimes it would take us an hour to get her to take all her medicine.

To help with the situation, a child life specialist at Children's National Medical Center in Washington suggested a system she often uses with children. For every dose Olivia took within five minutes of its scheduled time, she received $1 in play money. For every shot, she received two of the faux bills. At the end of each week, Olivia could use her savings to purchase toys.

Initially, I wasn't happy about how high the specialist priced the toys. Here was my child, isolated in a hospital room, suffering from a dreadful illness, and she was supposed to pay $25 in play money for a Barbie doll that would ordinarily cost just $5 in real money. If anybody deserved a discount, I thought, it was Olivia.

Good thing I didn't say anything. If I had, I would have let my sympathy for Olivia ruin an opportunity for her to practice some important lessons in personal finance. As parents, we need to understand that our children are capable at a young age of understanding basic concepts about money.

As the child specialist explained, if the toys were priced too low, Olivia would have little incentive to take all her medication. She was right: If we made it too easy for Olivia to earn the play money, she wouldn't have to save up to pay for what she wanted.

The reward system turned out to be a blessing. Olivia began taking her medicine with much more ease. The money lesson was a wonderful bonus.

I watched as Olivia put off buying a lot of smaller, less expensive items. Instead, she chose to bank her money so she could purchase items that she really wanted but that cost more. She even decided once to use almost her entire week's worth of earnings to buy a Bob the Builder play set for her brother and a doll for her sister.

It was gratifying to see that even during such a trying time, Olivia applied the following principles that my husband and I teach her at home:

- The sense of accomplishment that comes from earning your own money, even just play money.

- The importance of waiting and saving for what you want.

- The understanding that you can't always afford to buy everything you want.

- The pleasure you get when you use your money to make someone else happy.

There is no guarantee that if you teach your children the right things, they will become good money managers. But the odds are better if you don't just leave it up to teachers in the classroom.

## DON'T RAISE MATERIAL BOYS AND GIRLS

As any parent knows, children will get on your last nerve with all their nagging for more stuff. In a poll commissioned by the Center for a New American Dream, the average twelve- to seventeen-year-old will nag nine times to get a product his or her parent refuses to purchase. About half the parents give in at the end of all that pestering, the poll showed.

But deep down what children crave can't be satisfied with a trip to the mall. It can't be bought.

In an essay contest sponsored by the center, kids were asked, "What do you really want that money can't buy?"

More than two thousand children responded to the contest. Here's what Erika, fourteen, said: "My parents love me and buy me many things. I do things with my mom a lot, but my dad works and sleeps. I know we need the money, but I wish he would do more things with me."

Nearly six out of ten kids age nine through fourteen said they'd rather spend time having fun with their parents than go shopping at the mall.

Almost a quarter of the children interviewed said their parents were too busy working to spend time with them. Perhaps most revealing was the fact that only 13 percent of the children polled said they wished their parents made more money.

Fifty-eight percent of the children said they felt pressured to buy things in order to fit in.

People at all levels are upgrading their lifestyles, taking on more debt, and, in the process, often unintentionally teaching their children to do the same.

But maybe it's time you spent more time and less money to give your child something money can't buy. That's the best way to raise good money managers.

I learned to be a smart consumer, and the beauty of keeping things simple, from my grandmother. In fact, Big Mama wouldn't buy me stuff as a child even when I knew she could afford it.

"Child, I don't want you to have it better than I did," she would say.

That sounded selfish and nonsensical to me.

But Big Mama had a point.

"If I give you everything you want or what your friends have, then how will you learn to live on what you make?" Big Mama would ask. "How will you learn to appreciate the things that really matter?"

Even if you and your husband have the money, hold back a little from giving your children so much stuff.

Be a penny-pincher even when you don't have to. Every year I hold a contest within my *Washington Post* column. I received hundreds of entries for the Penny Pincher of the Year Contest, from the tried and true (reusing plastic bags) to the disgusting (bathing in someone else's used bathwater is just not right, and it's not sanitary) to smart saving strategies (sisters a year apart sharing the same high school ring).

My friends and family believe that if I didn't run this contest, I would win it.

I once stopped at a fast-food restaurant to get something to eat for a road trip. Not long after I pulled away from the drive-through, I got into an accident. My car flipped over several times.

Now, most normal people would have been praying or watching their life flash before their eyes. Not this penny-pincher. The whole time I was rolling over, I was watching my food roll around me, thinking, *Darn, there goes my seven-dollar lunch. Shoot, maybe when the car stops I could still salvage my fries or the hamburger.*

I once found a way to save on birthday cake, which often goes half eaten. My husband and son have the same first name, and their birthdays are just a month apart.

When it came time for my husband to cut his cake—his birthday comes first—I refused to let him cut the part that said HAPPY BIRTHDAY KEVIN, written in green icing. When the party was over, I wrapped up the cake and stored it in the freezer. A month later I thawed the cake to use for my son's birthday party.

I tried to use leftover icing to cover the sliced section, but it kept sliding off. Still, I put on the appropriate six candles (recycled, of course) for my son and served the remainder of the cake.

I was teased unmercifully. But I didn't pay the partygoers any mind.

Why? Because my son didn't care that half the cake was missing. He didn't even notice. He just wanted a cake with his name on it.

Too many parents treat their little children as if they are royalty who deserve everything they want. And yet when it comes time to send them to get a college education—something many of them will need—they don't have the money.

I often hear parents say they search for the perfect gifts for their kid's birthday, Christmas, or Hanukkah because they want to show him or her how much they care. Gifts shouldn't be viewed that way. Gifts should be given to show that you care, not how much.

Could a PlayStation, Game Boy, Barbie Cruise Ship, or whatever the latest toy craze is really measure how much you care for your child? And if so, if you don't buy all that stuff—if you don't find the perfect present—does that mean you don't care?

As parents, we live for the "wow factor." You know what I mean, right? It's the moment your child opens her gift and her little eyes become extra wide with excitement and she shrieks, "Wow!" However, at some point I realized that the glee children feel as they rip open gift after gift is temporary.

I'd rather put my money toward something that is really going to last for my child—like a college education. In my house, every time one of my kids asks for something and it's not in the budget, I say, "I have two words for you—*college fund*." They ask for toys I know they won't play with, and I say, "I've got two words for you—*college fund*." When they try to embarrass me in a store into buying them something they don't need, I tell them again, "Two words—*college fund*."

You do right by your children by setting priorities for your money. That's why budgeting is so important. When you budget, all your money is spoken for, so you can say no to most unnecessary purchases. In my house, every time one of my children asks for something and it's not in the budget, I have two words for them—*college fund*.

During one such exchange, Olivia kept asking for something (I don't even remember what it was). I kept saying over and over again: "Two words—*college fund*."

"Please, Mommy," she whined. "I know you have the money."

"You got that right. *I* have the money," I said. "Besides, I've got two words for you—*college fund*."

"Well, I have two words for you," Olivia said. *"Nursing home."*

# 24

---

# SAVE FOR COLLEGE
# TO AVOID SADDLING
# CHILDREN WITH DEBT

There is hardly any question that a college education, even if you have to borrow to pay for it, is worth the investment.

But many students and their parents have to ask themselves, *When does the borrowing become too burdensome?*

An estimated 39 percent of student borrowers are graduating with unmanageable levels of student loan debt, according to "The Burden of Borrowing," a report by the Higher Education Project of the State Public Interest Research Groups. Unmanageable student loan debt is defined as monthly payments exceeding 8 percent of a borrower's monthly income.

The average federal loan debt among student borrowers has nearly doubled in eight years, to $16,928, according to 1999–2000 data from the National Postsecondary Student Aid Study conducted by the Department of Education. Yet the average income of eighteen- to twenty-four-year-olds with bachelor's degrees working full-time and year-round in 2000 was $32,101, according to the U.S. Census Bureau. Taken together, the data suggest that people coming out of college are having to devote too much of their income to repaying higher-education loans.

"Too often debt burden becomes a ball and chain for student borrowers after graduation," Tracey King, the research group's higher-education associate, said in announcing the report.

Most of the findings of the report didn't come as a surprise. For example, 71 percent of low-income students (from families with incomes of $20,000 or less) graduate with debt, compared with 44 percent of students from families with incomes of $100,000 or more. Fifty-five percent of African-American and 58 percent of Hispanic student borrowers graduate with unmanageable levels of debt. But it is not just minority students who are feeling the debt squeeze.

In 1999–2000, 64 percent of students graduated with loan debt, compared with 42 percent in 1992–93. In addition, the number of seniors who graduated with more than $20,000 in debt increased from 5 percent in 1992–93 to 33 percent in 1999–2000.

But here's what I found most interesting in the report:

There has been a rapid increase in the percentage of wealthy students who borrow. The percentage of dependent students from families with incomes of $100,000 or more who took out loans quadrupled from 1992–93 to 1999–2000, from 11 percent to 44 percent. The percentage of those student borrowers whose families had incomes between $80,000 and $99,999 more than doubled—from 24 percent to 58 percent—over the same time.

The report found that low-income students on average needed to borrow $8,351 to attend college. On the other hand, wealthy students needed an average of only $2,520. But the latter group ended up borrowing on average $4,321 a year—or nearly $2,000 more than they needed.

Many middle- and upper-income parents complain that they make too much to qualify for grants or subsidized loans. Without such help, they protest, they can't afford to pay college costs. Some students and their families really do need to borrow, and affordable loans and grant money should be available.

But ask yourself: Is the reason your child has to take on so much debt because you can't afford to pay, or because you failed to manage your finances?

I'm not addressing the families or women who face various financial crises or don't earn enough to meet their basic needs. I'm talking about people with good incomes who choose not to save for their child's college education.

And it is a choice.

After a house, the next most expensive purchase for many families is a car. The average cost of a new car is $20,000. The average cost of a four-year public institution, including tuition, fees, and room and board, was about $11,354 during the 2004–2005 academic year, according to the College Board. It was $27,516 at a four-year private school.

Don't tell me you can't afford to pay for college if you bought a new car instead of a used one, or if your credit cards are near the maximum limit.

Do you think I'm being a little tough?

Good.

Maybe it will be the wake-up call you need to stop buying a new car every few years. Maybe you will curb your spending on clothes, entertainment, and eating out when you realize your lack of savings could saddle your child with burdensome college debt.

## BRAND NAME ISN'T ALWAYS BETTER

Are you and your husband fighting over whether your child needs to attend a brand-name college? If so, I've got some information that may help end at least this one conflict.

Thousands of parents and students approach the college search by forgetting they are consumers. Price matters.

In one survey, the American Council on Education asked people how parents generally approach the college decision. Given a choice between a very good, expensive college that would require major financial sacrifices and an average, less expensive college, what should parents do?

The majority of respondents said parents should go for the bargain deal.

When the question was turned around, however, and they were told it was their own child who was accepted at the higher-priced school, the answer changed. The majority would go straight for the brand name.

A brand name does not always mean a school is a better investment. As a matter of fact, there is a growing body of research that challenges the notion that the earning power of college graduates is greatly elevated by the more elusive and expensive schools.

Price, prestige, and pedigree are the three P's that matter to too many parents and students, says Robert Zemsky, a University of Pennsylvania professor and director of the university's Institute for Research on Higher Education. Zemsky believes parents need to become better shoppers of institutions and look at price sooner in the college selection process.

It's easy to understand why brand-name college shopping is so fashionable. If you are like me, I know you don't want your babies to be living off you for the rest of your life, so you want them to get the best education possible. There has been plenty of anecdotal, as well as scholarly, evidence that attending elite schools is the surest road to prosperity.

But now, thankfully, there's some counterevidence that supports discount college shopping, too.

A study by Alan B. Krueger of Princeton University and Stacy Berg Dale, a researcher at the Andrew W. Mellon Foundation, found that while students who attended selective schools do well after graduation, so do students who attended less selective schools. The critical issue is not so much the school as the student. The studies are showing that the drive and ambition that help your children get into an expensive college are the same drive and ambition that will help them become successful at any school they attend.

If you and your spouse are struggling and fighting about money, be assured that you don't have to pile on more debt to send Junior to a brand-name college.

If your kid is bright and motivated, he or she will likely do just fine financially.

# PART 3: THEN COMES THE BABY CARRIAGE

### What's the Bottom Line?

Here's what you should have learned from part 3:

✔ If you're having a baby, spend less time in the baby store and more time attending to some important financial decisions.

✔ If you want people to know how to care for you if you become incapacitated, get a living will. If you care about leaving your family in peace after you've been put to rest, get a will.

✔ Start saving for college while your child is in diapers.

✔ If you can't save for college *and* your retirement, then put your retirement first. Your child can borrow to go to college. For the most part, you can't borrow to retire.

✔ The best time to start teaching your children about money is when they are young and impressed with what you know. And whether you realize it or not, you are teaching your children about money every day, for better or worse.

✓ What children crave can't be satisfied with a trip to the mall. It can't be bought. It's your presence, not the presents, that is important.

✓ Don't be lured by the three Ps—price, prestige, and pedigree—into paying for a brand-name college when less expensive schools are just as good.

✓ Don't saddle your child with unmanageable debt.

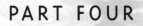

PART FOUR

# HOW YOU AND PRINCE CHARMING CAN SPEND WELL AND LIVE RICH

# 25

---

# WHEN YOU DON'T LIVE
# HAPPILY EVER AFTER

Here you are near the end of the book, and even now you know you're headed for divorce. There is no communication in your marriage. Compromise is a foreign concept. And the only common goal you and your husband have is finding the nearest exit.

At this point, you need a financial exit strategy.

Start collecting as much information as you can by reviewing documents kept in the house. Such papers include statements from your spouse's 401(k) plan, individual retirement accounts, investment statements, and bank accounts. Photocopy all the documents and store them in a safe place.

And you know where the best place is to find out about your family's finances?

Look at your joint tax return. If you can't find a copy of the return, order it from the Internal Revenue Service (www.irs.gov) using Form 4506, Request for Copy of Tax Return. Mail the form to the IRS address in the instructions along with a $39 fee for each tax year requested. Copies are generally available for returns filed in the current and past six years. You can request a photocopy of the actual return along with schedules and copies of W-2 forms. Or you can get a computer transcript with a line-by-line listing of the return information. The tax return transcript shows most line items contained on the original return, including any accompanying forms and schedules. The transcript can be ordered by completing a Form 4506-T or calling (800)829-1040 and following the prompts in the recorded message. There is no charge for the transcript; you should receive it in ten business days from the time the IRS receives your request. Tax return transcripts are generally available for the current and past three years.

You should also get a copy of your credit report from the three major credit reporting bureaus (see chapter 10). By combing through the credit report, you may find requests for joint credit cards, loans, or large purchases made by your spouse.

If you see statements coming in from financial institutions and banks and your name is on them, you have a right to open them.

And if a divorce is imminent—separate your finances completely!

I'm going to make this short and sweet for you. Here's basically what to consider when your marriage is over:

- You'll need to close joint accounts, or request that the creditor convert these accounts to individual accounts. Under the law, a creditor is prohibited from closing a joint account because of a divorce, but is permitted to do so if either spouse requests it. However, creditors are not *required* to change joint accounts to individual accounts. They can tell you to reapply for credit as an individual. Based upon the strength or weakness of your credit profile, they can either grant or deny credit.

- Don't forget to cancel other consumer credit card accounts, such as department store or gasoline accounts. Planning for the possibility of a divorce or death of a spouse means taking a long-term view. It makes sense, if you're married, to have at least one line of credit in your own name. That could provide some assurance, in a situation where all joint accounts or primary/authorized user accounts are suddenly made unavailable, that you would still have control over at least one line of credit.

Given the mutual benefit (or pain) that joint accounts can give both spouses, it's clear that early in a divorce proceeding, the spouses ideally should divide or split up their credit card accounts in whatever way makes sense. Not doing so leaves the door open for one spouse to abuse the joint accounts, resulting in financial problems for the other spouse, including possible harm to her credit rating.

- Not all assets are equal. Don't automatically and emotionally opt to keep the house, especially if you have no idea how you will make the monthly mortgage payments. Don't ignore retirement funds that may be worth more in the future given their tax benefits. As the Women's Institute for Financial Education (WIFE.org) points out, when deciding whether or not to keep the house, consider the cost of maintenance, repairs, homeowner's association fees, gardeners, and other household expenses. Although you may be able to afford the mortgage, the other expenses may exceed your budget.

- A divorce decree or settlement doesn't count for squat with a creditor. Many divorced women who negotiated to have their husbands pay off joint credit card debt or continue to make mortgage payments are shocked to learn that the settlement doesn't change their obligation to pay joint debts. Let me share an example with you from the Federal Trade

Commission. Mary and Bill recently divorced. Their divorce decree stated that Bill would pay the balances on their three joint credit card accounts. Months later, after Bill neglected to pay off these accounts, all three creditors contacted Mary for payment. She referred them to the divorce decree, insisting that she was not responsible for the accounts. The creditors correctly stated that they were not parties to the decree and that Mary was still legally responsible for paying off the couple's joint accounts. Mary later found out that the late payments appeared on her credit report.

Here's another story illustrating how important it is to cancel any joint credit cards you have when headed for a divorce: "When I was divorced, my ex-husband was to pay off all existing credit cards that were in our names, my name, and in his business's name. This was stated in our property agreement—a legal document. He paid all cards with both our names and in the name of the business, but the card that was in my name only he stopped paying a little after one year. It took forever for the credit card issuer to track me down, and by that time, the card payments were several months overdue. The balance was less than $1,000 and the overdue payments only added up to about $100. Anyway, once the creditors tracked me down, I paid the balance in full. I've got a credit blemish because the card company closed the account due to nonpayment and it shows that I paid it off through a collection company. Would the credit bureau consider changing my credit report if they were to see the legal document that said he was responsible for paying the payments? Or am I out of luck since the card was in my name only?"

I told the writer that her ex was a bum—but unfortunately the debt was technically hers. She was out of luck, although she could always try small claims court.

And look at this reader's question: "My husband and I have decided to separate, partly over financial issues. We recently bought a house. My name is on the mortgage and both names are on the title. We've agreed, orally, that I will keep the house because I'm the primary caretaker of our toddler. At what time should my husband's name be taken off the house title (he's amenable to that thus far)? Oh, and one more—should we put our agreements so far in writing while things are mostly amenable?" I advised this woman to find an attorney right away. It's not that things can't stay civil—but when the love goes, so can people's sense of right and wrong. Most important, she should do whatever she can to get her husband's name off the title so she can own it free and clear.

- Don't assume you will get 50 percent of everything. That's not necessarily so. According to Asset Dynamics, an investment advisory and financial planning firm, the standard in most, though not all, divorces is referred to as "equitable distribution." What that means, however, varies from state to state and even from judge to judge. *Equitable* does not mean "equal." Exactly how your assets will be divided depends on a number of factors, including the length of the marriage, income capacity, and so on. In the case of equitable distribution, everything you acquired during your marriage is subject to division.

- Only in the following community property states—Arizona, California, Idaho, Louisiana, New Mexico, Nevada, Texas, Washington, and Wisconsin—is there a fifty-fifty split in marital property.

- In community property states, just as assets are equally divided, so are debts. This means you can be held liable for debts accumulated during the marriage.

Here are seven key questions to ask about retirement benefits in the event of a divorce, according to the Equality in Marriage Institute:

1. Does your spouse have more than one pension or retirement plan from a current or previous job?

2. Has your spouse worked long enough to earn a legal right to the pension?

3. How much has been earned or "accrued" in pension benefits under each plan?

4. Do you need to have the benefit valued?

5. What information needs to be in the court order, decree, or property settlement before the pension plan will pay the benefits directly to you?

6. Does the order clearly specify what amount is to be paid to you?

7. Does the order provide for survivor benefits, so that your benefits can continue if your former spouse should die first?

While in marriage your goal should be to merge everything, in divorce it should be to separate everything.

# 26

---

# GETTING DOWN
# TO THE BASICS

George Orwell said that at fifty, everyone has the face he deserves. Can the same be said about your personal finances? At fifty and beyond, will you have the retirement you deserve?

One reader wasn't sure about his wife. He wrote: "I'm very concerned my wife has fallen way behind on her retirement savings. She is forty-eight and has a total of $6,000. What should she do?"

I definitely feel the fear of one single woman who is late to the retirement savings game. She wrote: "I am single with no children. What is the best way to save for retirement? I want to start with a Roth IRA but I'm not sure."

Or perhaps you are doing pretty well in the savings department but now you're not sure what else to do—like this couple: "We have no debt and have saved $20,000 in a money market account. What's next? Should we now be exploring other options? Or maybe we should head straight for a financial planner and make sure we're on all the right tracks?"

I'll talk about the right time to get a financial planner later on in this chapter. For now, I'll address the basic question of what comes next after you've saved your emergency money.

What's next is retirement. Actually, this should have been a major part of your financial plan from the beginning.

Workers and retirees are uncomfortable with how much they have accumulated during their pre-retirement years, according to the findings of a survey by OppenheimerFunds, a leading asset manager. Ninety-seven percent of workers in the Oppenheimer survey said that they regretted how they and their spouse spent their money considering how much more savings they could have accumulated; 98 percent of retirees regret how they spent their money before retiring.

But there's no need to look back over failed savings. What good is it going to do to blame yourself or your spouse for your overspending? However, once you realize you're behind in retirement savings, get busy. And the first thing you should do is get educated.

I think it's safe to say that a large percentage of the millions of individuals investing today really don't know what they are doing. The results of far too many surveys will back me up. When tested on their knowledge of investing, many people get a failing grade.

It's not that investors are stupid. It's just that the world of investing has become much more complex. The basics aren't so basic anymore.

In one study conducted by the Vanguard Group and *Money* magazine, one thousand randomly selected investors in eighteen states were asked to complete a twenty-question financial literacy test, which included questions on the fundamentals of mutual funds. On average, the investors got 60 percent of the questions wrong.

> "If a man empties his purse into his head, no one can take it away from him. An investment of knowledge always pays the best interest."
>
> **Benjamin Franklin**

There is a scripture in Proverbs that I think speaks to how we all should go about investing for our future, whether it's for retirement, a home, or a college fund. Proverbs 24:3–4 says: "Through wisdom a house is built, and by understanding it is established; by knowledge the rooms are filled with all precious and pleasant riches."

If you want to invest well and live rich, however complicated this stuff is, at least do a little homework to gain some understanding of investing. Because when it comes to investing, ignorance is not bliss. It can leave you broke.

I stay in the study mode because I can't trust that anyone else will really look out for my best financial interests. Even a little bit of knowledge will help you make better choices about how to invest your money.

To start, you should know that for most individual investors, the easiest, least risky way to invest is through mutual funds. A mutual fund is a portfolio of stocks, bonds, or money market securities that is owned by many investors and managed by a professional investment company. Unlike bank accounts, mutual funds are not insured or guaranteed by any government agency. If you're not interested in getting into some heavy-duty individual stock investing, the best way to save for your retirement is by buying into a mutual fund, either on your own or through an employer-sponsored retirement plan.

While there are now more retirement plan choices and more incentives to get individuals to save more for retirement, trying to figure out which to use when you have more options than money can be mind-boggling, according to CCH Inc., a provider of tax and pension law information. The basic retirement planning options open to most individuals include funding a traditional IRA; setting up a Roth IRA; and contributing to employer-sponsored plans, such as 401(k) plans.

Here are basic descriptions of each of those options:

## THE TRADITIONAL IRA

An IRA allows you to contribute money into a tax-deferred account and deduct your contribution from your current income taxes in many cases. If your employer doesn't offer a retirement plan, or if you're a nonworking spouse, you can use an IRA to save for your retirement. You set up one of these accounts and then decide what kind of investment will go into it, such as a stock fund or a bond mutual fund.

You can contribute up to $4,000 a year to an IRA through 2007. The contribution limit increases to $5,000 in 2008, and is indexed to inflation thereafter. Taxpayers age fifty and over have a special catch-up period that allows them to add another $1,000 per year beginning in 2006.

Contributions and earnings in an IRA grow tax-deferred until you begin withdrawals—usually not before age fifty-nine-and-a-half. Withdrawals are taxed as ordinary income in the year they are taken out of the account. In most cases, the IRS treats withdrawals before the age of fifty-nine-and-a-half as ordinary income and imposes a 10 percent penalty on top of that. With a traditional IRA, you have to take distributions by age seventy-and-a-half, and you can no longer contribute after this age.

IRAs cannot be owned jointly. A wife and husband must each

set up their own. However, any amount remaining in your IRA upon your death can be paid to your beneficiary or beneficiaries.

To be eligible to contribute to an IRA, you—or your spouse, if you file a joint return—must have taxable compensation, such as wages, salaries, commissions, tips, bonuses, or net income from self-employment. The income requirement does not include earnings and profits from property, such as rental income, interest and dividend income, or any amount received as pension or annuity income, or as deferred compensation.

Many people find their IRA contributions are fully deductible; however, if you or your spouse participates in an employer-sponsored retirement plan—a 401(k), for example—your IRA deduction may be reduced or eliminated. (Just a note: Technically, in the tax code, *IRA* stands for "individual retirement arrangement." However, financial institutions commonly call them "individual retirement accounts.")

You can contribute to an IRA up until the date your income taxes are due for that year. For example, you could fund an IRA by April 15, 2006, and deduct the contribution from your 2005 taxes. However, don't wait until tax day to open an IRA. The sooner in the year you invest, the quicker you have your money working for you.

## THE ROTH IRA

A Roth IRA differs from traditional IRAs in that contributions are not deductible. The amount you may contribute to a Roth IRA is gradually reduced if your modified adjusted gross income is between $95,000 and $110,000 if you are single; between $150,000 and $160,000 if you are married and file a joint return; and between $0 and $10,000 if you are married, live with your spouse, and file a separate return.

Roth IRAs have the same contribution limits as traditional IRAs. And just like a traditional IRA, if you are fifty or older you qualify for the catch-up contribution.

You can withdraw your contributions at any time without paying a penalty or taxes. In most cases, however, if you withdraw any earnings before the age of fifty-nine-and-a-half, a 10 percent penalty will be imposed if the account has been open for less than five years.

One of the benefits of a Roth is that you aren't forced to take distributions.

And changes in the tax code created a new option for investors beginning in 2006. Workers can now elect to have some or all of their deferrals in a 401(k) or 403(b) as after-tax contributions or Roth contributions. The new Roth 401(k) option will allow workers to contribute after-tax dollars up to the overall limit for 401(k) contributions. And there is no income cap for this option. Remember, the advantage of a Roth contribution is that all the money you withdraw is tax-free.

You will need to be careful how your retirement withholding is set up. If the amount withheld during the year puts you over the limit and the excess in the Roth 401(k) is not returned to you by the following April 15, you could face penalties.

## THE 401(k), 403(b), OR 457 PLAN

These are all "defined contribution plans," and they offer employees an opportunity to put pretax dollars into a selected group of investments, often mutual funds. Earnings in these accounts grow tax-deferred.

A 403(b) plan is similar to a 401(k) plan but is exclusively for employees who work for hospitals or health care organizations, charitable foundations, religious organizations, or educational institutions. There are two general types of 403(b) plans—tax-sheltered annuities issued by an insurer and custodial accounts in which an employee's money is invested in mutual funds. Either type of 403(b) plan allows participants to make pretax contributions. A 457 plan is set up for government workers.

When you invest in a 401(k) or similar plan, think of the account as a big pot. You will be deciding what investments to put into that pot.

For 2006, you can contribute up to $15,000. These annual deferral limits are indexed for inflation in $500 increments in 2007 and thereafter. These types of plan also have a catch-up provision. You can contribute another $5,000 per year if you are fifty or older for a total of $20,000.

Many employers will match an employee's contribution up to a certain limit. You definitely want to contribute enough money to capture your employer's match. Otherwise, you'd be walking away from free money.

Also keep in mind that early withdrawals from the plan (before age fifty-nine-and-a-half) are subject to an early-distribution penalty of 10 percent. You also have to pay ordinary income tax on the distributed money, unless an exception applies.

## THE ROTH VERSUS THE 401(k)

One of the most confusing decisions for many investors is whether to put money into a Roth or a 401(k).

If you invest in a Roth, you invest after-tax money, but your withdrawals are tax-free. With a 401(k) or similar plan, money goes in pretax, but you pay ordinary income taxes when you withdraw it.

So should you forgo the tax break of a 401(k) now in return for receiving tax-free distributions later, in which case you would opt for a Roth IRA?

The answer is: It depends.

Here are a few things to think about in making your decision:

- The 401(k) plans have two major advantages: They permit larger contributions, and employers often match a portion of the money you invest, which means an immediate return on your money. Generally, it's better to first contribute to a 401(k) plan, at least up to the highest amount that an employer will match, before making a contribution to a Roth IRA. Otherwise you are leaving a guaranteed pot of money on the table.

- Unlike a traditional IRA, a Roth IRA does not require that any distributions be taken. Therefore, it can be a powerful estate-planning tool if you don't need the money in retirement and would like to hold on to the tax deferral benefit for your heirs.

- If your employer offers a Roth 401(k), you may not have to choose between a 401(k) and a traditional Roth. Remember, the traditional Roth IRA cannot be used by people with incomes over $110,000 ($160,000 for a married couple). On the other hand, there is no income limit for a Roth 401(k).

- If your employer doesn't offer a Roth 401(k), keep in mind the importance of the contribution limits. If you contribute to a standard 401(k) and a Roth 401(k), your total contribution is higher than a traditional Roth—$15,000 compared with $6,000 at most (not including any inflation indexing). With the ability to put more money into a 401(k), you can have more money with the potential to earn a return and grow tax-free.

## MANAGED VERSUS INDEX

What's the difference between an actively managed fund and an index fund?

Don't know? Don't feel bad. Many investors don't know the difference.

In an actively managed fund, a fund manager tries to outperform similar funds or a certain market benchmark, such as Standard & Poor's 500 Stock Index (S&P 500). The S&P consists of five hundred of the most widely held companies traded on the New York and American stock exchanges and the over-the-counter (OTC) market. This index tracks companies in leading industries such as transportation, utilities, financial services, and technology.

Active mutual fund managers use research, market forecasts, and their own judgment and experience to buy and sell securities.

Index funds, sometimes called "passively managed funds," don't try to beat the market. Instead, managers of index funds seek to track closely the performance of a target market index. Index funds buy and hold all, or a representative sample, of the securities in the index.

So which kind of fund is better—an actively managed fund or an index fund?

Both can play a role in an investment portfolio. Some investors who seek to outpace the market favor actively managed funds. However, such funds may also perform worse than the market average—and they often do.

Other investors prefer the greater consistency of index funds because their performance tracks more closely that of market benchmarks than does the performance of actively managed funds.

Whatever you decide, it's smart to diversify among different types of investments, and often that means diversifying among mutual fund companies as well.

## BASICALLY SPEAKING

Whatever you do, don't end up with what some experts call "paralysis by analysis"—meaning you invest very little or not at all because you are unable to decide what to do. Follow these four basic tips for investing and you will do well:

1. Invest for the long term—at least five years. If you will need your money in less than five years, don't invest it in anything. While you may get a higher return by investing than you would in a simple savings account, you also risk losing all your money. Can you afford that?

2. Diversify. You have not diversified if you own shares in three different small-cap funds (mutual funds specializing in the stocks of companies whose market value is less than $1 billion). Small-cap company stocks are generally more volatile than the stocks of mid-cap or large-cap companies. Make sure even if you are investing in mutual funds that you don't over-expose yourself by using the same type of mutual fund. The name of this game is to not have all your financial eggs in one basket.

3. When in doubt, invest in balanced funds. Such funds provide some combination of growth, income, and conservation of

capital by investing in a mix of stocks, bonds, and/or money market instruments.

4. Understand the tax implications of your fund and how fees can affect your return. Only 21 percent of the investors in a Vanguard survey knew that if your fund charges an expense ratio (management fee) of 1 percent, your returns are reduced by 1 percent each year you own it. (Expense ratios typically range from 0.2 to 2 percent.) A fee difference of 1 percent for a $10,000 investment earning 8 percent annually can reduce that investment's value by $7,000 over a twenty-year period. Taxes are one of the most significant costs of investing in a mutual fund. You need to pay attention to this because if there is a lot of buying and selling in the fund, it could generate capital gains taxes for you. That means you might have to pay taxes on those gains even if you didn't sell any shares in the mutual fund itself—and even if the fund is down for the year. To find a mutual fund's after-tax return, look in its prospectus.

## MANAGING RETIREMENT, AUTOMATICALLY

Automation can be a wonderful thing.

Take, for example, the introduction of the automatic fabric-softener dispenser on washing machines. I remember a time when you had to rush back to the washer to pour in the fabric softener. Even having a buzzer didn't help me because I often got busy and didn't hear it.

My curling iron automatically shuts off, which I'm sure has saved me from burning down my house.

Thankfully, in a similar vein, investors can now select mutual funds that automatically adjust their investment portfolios. This fund option is called "life cycle investing," and its increasingly being offered in employer-sponsored retirement plans. There are two types of life cycle funds: "lifestyle" and "target date" or "target retirement."

"The appeal of both lifestyle and target retirement funds is that, with fund management companies managing allocations, investors can concentrate on other things," said Michael Porter and Lucas Garland, research analysts for Lipper Inc., in their 2005 report "Life Cycle Funds: Fit for Life."

With a lifestyle fund, investors choose funds based on how much risk they wish to take. The fund choices may vary from aggressive (80 percent stock) to conservative (20 percent stock) or somewhere in between. While the actual asset mix may vary from time to time, the asset allocation remains within a specific range.

A target date fund allocates the money you invest according to a preset schedule based on your target retirement date. The longer you have until retirement, the more aggressive the fund may be, because you have more time to ride the ups and downs of stocks, Porter and Garland said.

As with all investment strategies, there are some pros and cons to life cycle funds.

### *The cons:*

- Many of the funds, specifically the target date funds, use age as the overriding factor in determining how much of your money to put in stocks, bonds, and cash.

- Investors are likely to neglect a fund's performance because everything is automatic. Investing in a life cycle fund doesn't mean you shouldn't keep an eye on returns.

- Fee overload. When you buy a life cycle fund, you pay the fees charged for the underlying funds. However, some fund companies add a charge on top of that. Watch the fees, which eat into your returns.

## The pros:

- Surveys show people who participate in employer-sponsored retirement plans often don't change their asset allocations once they sign up because they don't know what to do. Life cycle funds put the decision on how to allocate your contributions in the hands of professionals.

- Investors can avoid common mistakes such as not diversifying enough or being too conservative in their early working life.

A life cycle fund has the simplification and automation many investors desperately need. Think of it as being like the automatic rotisserie oven hawked by infomercial king Ron Popeil. Set it and, for the most part, forget it.

## MISTAKES TO AVOID WHEN INVESTING IN BONDS

Bonds used to be boring.

Stocks were the sexy thing. Many investors saw them as their route to early retirement.

Of course, many people realize that bonds are the tortoises up against the stock market's hares.

Bonds may not give you as fast or as high a return as some hotshot stocks, and even pokier stocks will edge bonds out over a long period of time, but slow and steady can keep you in the race without giving you a heart attack.

Still, bonds can lose money. If you aren't careful, the bonds you buy can be riskier than you may want and cost more than you intended, according to financial planners from the Zero Alpha Group (ZAG), a network of seven national independent fee-only investment advisory firms.

Many people think that when they put money in bonds, they are investing risk-free. That's just not the case. Here are some common bond-investing mistakes:

• **Failing to consider buying a bond index fund:** You can invest in bond index funds just like stock index funds. With a bond index fund, professional money managers design a portfolio to match the performance of a particular broad-based bond index. For example, the Vanguard Total Bond Market Index Fund tracks the performance of the entire U.S. investment-grade taxable bond market.

• **Investing in long-term bonds when short-term might be better:** The longer the term of a bond, the more its return is tied to the swings of interest rates. For instance, let's say you buy a thirty-year bond at 3 percent interest. But ten years into the bond, interest rates rocket to 8 percent. New investors are now able to buy bonds at the higher interest rate while you're earning just 3 percent. Consider short-term bonds so that if interest rates rise, you won't have to wait as long to reinvest at higher yields.

• **Ignoring the tax man:** Interest from bonds is taxable at your normal income tax rate. Some bonds, however, offer special tax advantages. For example, there is no state or local income tax on the interest from U.S. Treasury bonds. There is also no federal income tax on the interest from most municipal bonds. In many cases, you also won't owe any state or local income tax, according to the Bond Market Association. The decision about whether to invest in a taxable bond or a tax-exempt bond can depend on whether the bonds will be held in an account that is already tax-preferred or tax-deferred, such as a pension account, 401(k), or individual retirement account. Investors in higher income tax brackets should consider keeping their taxable bonds in a tax-deferred account.

• **Chasing returns:** Remember the late 1990s. People chased stocks all over the map hoping to strike gold. And some did. However, most just found fool's gold. For every person who got in at the right time on a rising stock, there are four or five more who chased a stock at the wrong time. Chasing bonds to bolster portfolio performance during a volatile stock market can be just as risky as stock chasing.

• **Buying too much junk:** The types of bonds you can buy range from the highest-credit-quality U.S. Treasury securities, which are backed by the full faith and credit of the U.S. government, to bonds that are below investment grade and considered speculative (junk bonds). Since a bond may not mature for years—even decades—credit quality is important. Small individual investors need to realize that junk bonds that promise returns of 7 percent, 10 percent, or more in a 1 percent or 2 percent interest rate environment are riskier because the company issuing the bond may not be financially strong. And you need to keep an eye on the bond's rating, which can be downgraded, making the bond riskier. Institutional investors often use junk bonds in their portfolios to great advantage—mainly because they are able, by virtue of their much larger portfolios, to invest in more company debt, thereby reducing their risk.

It took a downturn in the stock market for bonds to get the respect and attention they deserve. But don't rush to bonds without first understanding their role in your investment portfolio for the long term.

## CHOICES FOR CONSERVATIVE SAVERS

When it came to investing, my grandmother had one strategy: Protect your principal. She put all of her money into a passbook savings account. She didn't invest in stocks. The only bond she ever bought was the adhesive material that held her dentures in place.

Big Mama believed you could build wealth without Wall Street.

When she died, she wasn't a wealthy woman. But she had managed to amass enough money to take care of her financial needs during her retirement.

I never succeeded in getting my grandmother to put her money anywhere but in a simple savings account. But there are other virtually risk-free choices that will give you a bit more return on your money.

The first time I sat down with my financial planner, she asked me to describe my "risk tolerance." If you're not familiar with that term, it means: How comfortable are you with the possibility of losing any or all of your money if you choose certain investment options? For example, junk bonds are highly risky. If you decide to invest in them, you should have a high tolerance for risk. On the other end of the risk scale is the ultrasafe U.S. savings bond.

Where do you fall on the risk scale? Are you the kind of person who thinks twice about putting a quarter in a gumball machine because you're scared that when you turn the little knob, your gumball might not drop and you would lose your quarter? If so, you have a very low risk tolerance.

I'm happy if I can protect my principal and guard against inflation, which means making sure the money I save today can buy the same amount of goods or services in the future.

If you're risk-averse, you may be interested in two inflation-indexed securities offered by the U.S. Treasury: Treasury Inflation-Protected Securities (TIPS) and I Bonds. Both are designed for investors who want a guaranteed rate of return on their principal and inflation protection.

With TIPS, introduced in 1997, the principal amount invested is adjusted for inflation using the consumer price index. Interest is paid semiannually and is calculated using the adjusted principal amount.

Like other notes and bonds, TIPS pay a fixed rate of interest. But that rate is applied to the inflation-adjusted principal. So if inflation occurs throughout the life of your security, every interest payment will be greater than the previous one. However, in the event of deflation (a decline in overall prices), your interest payments will decrease. Yet even if there is a period of deflation, you are guaranteed a return of your original principal.

"With TIPS, you have a lot of protection against rising inflation and interest rates, which you don't have in a normal bond, and that's the scary thing about just locking in normal bonds right now with rates so low," said Michael W. Boone, a certified financial planner from Bellevue, Washington. "Also, TIPS are extremely liquid. They are very easy to buy and sell. But you get whatever the market price is, so you may get more or less than what you put in if you sell them before maturity."

You can buy TIPS directly from the Treasury in July, October, and January in multiples of $1,000. The only maturity available is ten years. You can buy TIPS at any time in the secondary market.

TIPS are exempt from state and local income taxes, but they are subject to federal income tax. You will have to pay taxes each year on any gains, on the interest earned and the inflation-adjusted principal amount. You can avoid paying the taxes each year if you hold TIPS in a tax-deferred account such as an individual retirement account. For more details about TIPS or purchasing information, go to www.treasurydirect.gov.

The second type of inflation-protected Treasury security is the Series I inflation-indexed savings bond, which was introduced in 1998. The I Bond is an accrual-type security, meaning interest is added to the bond monthly and paid when the bond is cashed. The bonds are sold at face value—you pay $100 for a $100 bond.

The earnings rate is a combination of a fixed interest rate plus the rate of inflation, adjusted semiannually. The fixed rate remains the same throughout the life of the bond, while the semiannual inflation rate can be changed every six months. Both the fixed rate of return and the semiannual inflation rate are announced by the Treasury Department each May and November.

You can buy I Bonds from most banks, credit unions, and savings institutions, or on the Internet at www.savingsbonds.gov. You can invest as little as $50 or as much as $30,000 a year.

With an I Bond, you can defer federal taxes on earnings for up to thirty years. The bonds are also exempt from state and local income taxes.

Clearly, you won't get rich putting your money in TIPS or I Bonds. However, at least you will keep pace with inflation. Inflation decreases your dollars' value. If you are planning for your financial needs in the future, you'll need to protect the purchasing power of your money.

But if losing even a quarter bothers you, these two investment options will keep your money safe and sound. Ultimately, if you choose to stay off the road that leads to Wall Street, just be fore-warned that you'll need to save a lot of money for a long time so that the effect of compounding can make up for your conservative investing.

## ANNUITIES ALERT

The Securities and Exchange Commission (SEC) and NASD have three words for investors purchasing variable annuities: *Watch your back.* Okay, the two agencies didn't exactly say that, but that's essentially what a report by the two organizations recommends.

Variable annuity products combine features of insurance and securities investments. While variable annuities are appropriate for some, be careful if you're considering investing in these products. They are complex, with language and fee structures nearly impossible for the average consumer to understand.

The SEC and NASD (formerly the National Association of Securities Dealers) found in an examination of the way variable annuities are sold that brokers often make unsuitable recommendations to senior citizens and to individuals unable to afford the products without mortgaging their homes. Brokers also failed to disclose fully various fees or risks and overstated the tax benefits associated with annuities.

In one complaint to the SEC that I was allowed to review (minus any identifying information), an elderly couple produced an e-mail in which a salesperson told them that having an annuity as part of their tax-deferred investment account (an individual retirement account, or IRA) was the same as a "double tax-deferred investment."

That's utter nonsense. It's true that one key benefit to purchasing variable annuities is that earnings on the invested money ac-cumulate tax-deferred. "But purchasing a variable annuity within a tax-advantaged account will provide no additional tax savings," said Susan Wyderko, the director of the SEC's Office of Investor Education and Assistance. "It will, however, generate fees and commissions for the securities salesperson."

The report also found that firms repeatedly went back to the same customers and switched them to a new variable annuity product every few years, while a new annuity may impose higher fees and may reduce your death benefit, and you may have to pay a "surrender charge" on the old product, according to Wyderko.

A surrender charge is what you have to pay if you withdraw money from a variable annuity within a certain period after your purchase (typically within six or eight years, but sometimes as long as ten). Generally, the surrender charge is a percentage of the amount withdrawn, and the percentage declines gradually over time. Some contracts will allow you to withdraw part of your ac-count value each year—10 percent or 15 percent, for example—without paying a surrender charge.

In another complaint to the SEC, one woman described her discovery that if she wanted to get out of her annuity, it would cost her a $4,400 surrender charge. And that was actually the first time she realized she had invested in such a product. This seventy-year-old woman had thought she was rolling over $98,000 from a 401(k) plan into a mutual fund.

"Under no circumstances did I want anything that I couldn't get out of in a year—two at the most," she wrote in her SEC com-plaint. "I was in total shock as my investment had lost approxi-mately $12,000 [and] I was tied into an annuity for seven years. This was my first inkling of having invested in an annuity."

High fees and surrender charges combined with other factors make variable annuities inappropriate for many investors. So before purchasing such an investment product, the SEC and NASD recommend that you answer the following questions:

- Will you need the money in the next few years? Variable annuities are long-term investment vehicles. If you even vaguely think you'll need the money in the short term, don't go this route.

- Do you have enough money right now to purchase this product? It's downright dangerous to your financial health to mortgage your home in order to purchase a variable annuity or variable life insurance product. If a salesperson pressures you to do so, call the SEC at (800)732-0330.

- Are you being told to purchase a variable annuity or variable insurance as part of your IRA, SEP-IRA, Keogh, or other tax-deferred retirement account? Remember, those products already have a tax advantage.

- How much are the fees? Variable annuities have high commissions, typically above 5 percent. The annual fees on variable annuities can reach 2 percent or more of the annuity's value, according to NASD. So do not sign any paperwork until you know exactly what fees and expenses you will have to pay.

For more information about variable annuities, read the SEC's "Variable Annuities: What You Should Know" at www.sec.gov/investor/pubs/varannty.htm. Also check out "Variable Annuities: Beyond the Hard Sell" at www.nasd.com/Investor/Alerts/alert_variable_annuities.htm and "Should You Exchange Your Variable Annuity?" at www.nasd.com/Investor/Alerts/alert_annuity exchanges.htm.

A variable annuity may make sense for people who have con-

tributed the maximum to a 401(k) and other before-tax retirement plans, who don't need the money for a long time, and who
want an investment product with a death benefit and a payout option that can provide income for life. As you can see, those are a
lot of conditions. But please don't buy a variable annuity without
doing some research. There are just too many complex features
and fees that you need to watch out for.

## DON'T FORGET: LIFE IS IMPORTANT
## (LIFE INSURANCE, THAT IS)

Without a doubt, life insurance is something you need. But it can
be a pain to purchase and understand. A survey by the National
Association of Insurance Commissioners found that only 28 percent of people with insurance—life, auto, home, health, or disability—really understood the details of their coverage.

There are two types of life insurance. First, there is "term" life
insurance. With term life, you purchase a set amount of coverage
for a specified period of time, after which the premium can be adjusted depending on your health and age. If you miss a payment,
the policy may be canceled.

The other type of life insurance is "permanent" life. The biggest
selling point of permanent life is the cash value it can accumulate.
Permanent policies are known by a variety of names: whole, ordinary, universal, adjustable, and variable. If you're thinking about
purchasing permanent insurance, such as Variable Universal Life
policy (VUL), here are your basic choices, according to the American Council of Life Insurers:

• **Whole life or ordinary life:** Whole life policies stretch the cost
of insurance out over a longer period to level out the otherwise in-

creasing cost of the premiums. Part of your premium is used to pay for the death benefit, and the rest is invested by the insurance company, which is where the cash value comes from. Eventually you can use some of the cash buildup to pay the insurance premium. You can also borrow against the policy.

• **Universal life or adjustable life:** This kind of policy allows you, after your initial payment, to pay premiums at any time, subject to certain minimums and maximums. This type of policy usually guarantees a modest interest rate. A portion of each premium payment is used to pay for the insurance, some is used to pay fees, and the rest goes into a cash account. This type of policy is interest-rate sensitive. The cash value grows more in a higher-interest-rate environment.

• **Variable life:** This type of policy combines a death benefit with a cash value. The premium you pay (again, less certain fees such as commissions, investment management fees, and administrative charges) is invested. You can allocate your money among a variety of investments (typically mutual funds that invest in stocks, bonds, money market instruments, or some combination of the three). Anyone selling this type of insurance must be registered to sell securities with the Securities and Exchange Commission. The cash value is not guaranteed and grows according to how well your investment choices fare.

• **VUL:** This is a hybrid of universal and variable policies. Its main attraction is as a tax shelter. Under current tax law, investment earnings of VULs and other cash-value policies are not taxable if the policy is held until death. But an array of VUL charges can more than offset the advantage of this insurance product. Buying a VUL comes down to asking yourself three questions: *Do*

*I want permanent insurance? Do I want flexible premiums?* And *Do I want an investment vehicle attached to my policy?* If you answered yes to all three, then a VUL could be right for you.

Whichever type of insurance you choose, here's the most important tip: Don't use the insurance salesperson as your only source of information.

Would you ask only your grocer which foods and how much to buy for your family? I hardly think so. Certainly get advice from your insurance agent, but also do your own research.

There are so many good independent resources on the Internet. If you don't have a computer, go to the nearest public library. Many allow you free Internet access.

Not sure when you need life insurance? Try using this gauge:

• **For a child:** I know the death of a child would be devastating to you. However, his or her death most likely wouldn't be financially devastating. If you're worried about paying for the funeral if the unthinkable does happen, then start a small savings account. If you're disciplined enough to pay $20 a month for a small life insurance policy, why not just put that money in the bank? Even $20 a month earning just 2 percent in a simple savings account would grow to $6,268 in twenty-one years. Buying a life insurance policy for a child is a waste of money.

• **Single, no children, and no other dependents:** You don't need to worry about buying life insurance. Life insurance is meant to replace income that won't be coming in when you're dead. If you're a single woman and the only person depending on your salary is you, you don't need life insurance. Worried about your bills? Why? Unless a relative or friend has cosigned for any of your purchases, which would leave them with the bills to pay, don't sweat about your debts. If you are concerned about burdening your family with funeral costs, then buy a small policy to help pay for that expense. But again, a better use of your money is to set aside your burial fund in a savings account. Get someone you trust (Mom, Dad, or a favorite older relative) to be the cosigner on the account and tell them the money is to be used to pay for your funeral expenses. If you get a joint savings account, the money in the account won't be part of your estate since it will go to the joint account holder upon your death.

• **Single with children:** In this case, you absolutely need life insurance. If your children rely on your income, it's critical that you get a policy.

• **Married, no children:** Think about what your spouse will need after you're gone. Do you have a mortgage and other household expenses that take two incomes to pay each month? If so, you might want to get some life insurance if you don't want your other half to worry about having a roof over his head.

• **Married with children:** You are in the same category as the single mother with children. You should buy insurance to cover the income that won't be coming in once you're gone.

• **Stay-at-home mom:** The temptation here is to just buy life insurance for your husband, especially if money is tight. Wrong move. Think about how much it would cost to have someone take care of your children, including cleaning, cooking, and chauffeuring. See what I mean? It will take a lot of money to replace the services a stay-at-home parent renders for free.

• **Married, not far from retirement, children are grown:** Once the children are out of college and living on their own, you should evaluate your insurance needs. You should still consider the expenses your spouse will have in case you die, but if you've been saving and you have a nice nest egg (a pension, Social Security, retirement savings in taxable or tax-deferred accounts), you won't need life insurance.

## TERM IS BEST

This comment from a reader made me think: "Term life insurance has always seemed to be a waste of money to me," she wrote. "I get nothing at the end of the term."

Term life provides protection for a specific period of time, typically one to thirty years. It pays a death benefit only if you die during the term of the policy. Some policies can be automatically renewed at the end of the coverage period, and some can be converted to permanent insurance without any need for a medical exam.

Many people prefer permanent life insurance, also known as a "whole life" or "cash-value" policy, because it builds up that cash value. While the permanent policy is in force, you can borrow against it or use the accumulated value to pay premiums.

So, knowing that, is term a bad deal? No.

Term allows you to buy the most amount of insurance for the least amount of money. Term is like renting insurance, while permanent is like buying it. I often hear people say that when you rent rather than buy a home, you aren't getting anything back for your money.

But in fact you *are* getting something in return—a roof over your head. It's not as if you're going to live on the street until you can afford to buy a house. Renting isn't always a bad deal if that's what you want or all you can afford.

The same is true with term life insurance. For many people, term insurance is all that's needed.

If you do buy term, the Insurance Information Institute has listed the basic types of policy that are available:

• **Renewable term:** This kind of policy has a provision allowing you to renew coverage at the end of the term without having to show evidence of insurability. The company has to renew your policy even if your health has deteriorated. But the premium rate can rise with each renewal.

• **Level term:** This kind of policy provides a fixed premium for a certain number of years, usually ten or twenty, while the death benefit remains unchanged. The advantage is that you lock in a certain rate for a certain period of time. The disadvantage is that the premiums will tend to cost more than those charged in the earlier years of a renewable policy.

• **Decreasing term:** The death benefit in this kind of policy decreases over its term. For example, you might start with $100,000 of coverage, with the amount decreasing by $10,000 each year for ten years. The premium usually remains the same over the term of the policy. Decreasing the death benefit allows you to keep the premium the same as you grow older.

• **Increasing term:** With this kind of policy, the death benefit gradually increases over the life of the policy. You may start with a $100,000 policy and increase the death benefit $10,000 each year for ten years. The premium will also increase each year. This kind of policy may be appropriate if you see your insurance needs growing in coming years because, say, you expect to have more children.

One feature to consider when buying term is a convertible option. Premiums for convertible policies are usually higher than for nonconvertible policies. Once the policy is converted, the premiums for the permanent coverage will be higher than those of the term policy if you keep the same death benefit.

I know that buying life insurance is one of life's big annoyances. But if purchased correctly, it can be a great benefit to your survivors.

## IS IT TIME TO HIRE SOME FINANCIAL HELP?

> "Money and time are the heaviest burdens of life, and . . . the unhappiest of all mortals are those who have more of either than they know how to use."
>
> **Samuel Johnson**

Are you unhappy because you don't know what to do with your money? Maybe it's time to hire a financial planner. But first, what do you know about financial planners? Well, let's put you to the test:

### Financial Planning Fact or Fiction Quiz

1. True or false? Financial planners are the same as stockbrokers.

   Answer: False. The primary function of a stockbroker, insurance agent, or other financial salesperson is to sell you a financial product. It's understandable that you might be confused because, these days, just about anybody and his mama can call themselves a financial planner. Therefore, a stockbroker or insurance agent may also be a financial planner. But a good financial adviser's primary job is to help you identify your financial goals and work with you to develop a plan to reach those goals.

2. True or false? A financial planner is primarily an investment adviser.

Answer: False. Giving investment advice is just one part of what a financial planner does. Financial planners are supposed to help you look at your big financial picture—your debts, taxes, retirement savings, college savings for your children, estate planning, and insurance needs. Think of a financial adviser as a custom-home builder. He or she listens to your wishes and then designs the financial house that best suits you.

3. True or false? Only the rich can afford to hire a financial planner.

Answer: False. Different planners have different requirements as to whom they will take on as a client. Obviously, many look for high-income or high-net-worth individuals. But an increasing number of financial planners are working with modest-income clients. The industry is trying to bring its services to different income levels in society. One place to find a planner is through the Financial Planning Association; go to www.fpanet.org.

4. True or false? Financial planners aren't worth the money.

Answer: False. Sometimes good advice comes at a price. If you had an infected tooth, would you try to get it fixed free

by your uncle Buck or some other friend or relative? Hope-
fully not. And yet people think nothing of trying to get free
advice about something as important as their finances from
co-workers, neighbors, friends, and family. Still, I do understand the hesitation to pay for financial advice. It just
seems counterintuitive to pay good money to have someone
tell you what to do with your money. But a financial planner
can help you budget better or help you find ways to reduce
your taxes, boost your investment returns, or prevent a
costly financial catastrophe.

5. True or false? You should always hire a fee-only planner.
   Answer: False, with a caveat. Generally, if you want a planner who has no incentive to sell you any particular financial
   product, go with a fee-only planner. At hourly rates that
   can start at $100, however, fee-only planners can be expen-
   sive. Financial advisers earn their money in a variety of
   ways. Here are several methods of compensation, as outlined by the Financial Planning Association:

   • **Fee only:** Compensation can include an hourly fee, annual
   retainer, or percentage of assets managed. Fee-only planners
   do not earn commissions or fees on the products, investments, or recommendations they make. To find a fee-only
   planner, you might first check with the National Association
   of Personal Financial Advisors, which is the professional association of fee-only financial planners. Go to www.napfa.org,
   or call (800) 366-2732.

   • **Commission only:** There is no charge for the planner's advice or preparation of a financial plan. Compensation is received solely from the sale of financial products you agree

to purchase. Be careful about advisers who are paid based on what they sell you. You could be steered to higher-cost products that generate higher commissions for the planner.

• **Combination fee and commission:** A fee is charged for consultation, advice, and/or a financial plan. In addition, the planner may receive commissions from the sale of recommended products.

Whichever way you go, just be sure you fully understand how your financial planner is paid.

6. True or false? I can develop a financial plan on my own. Answer: True and false. If you're good at planning your financial future, you may not need the help of a financial adviser. But be honest with yourself. If you don't have the time or the inclination to figure out how best to use your money, hire a financial planner. Remember, prosperity often comes after much planning.

## SOMETIMES A MORTGAGE IS WORTH PAYING SLOWLY

My grandmother couldn't wait to pay off her mortgage. Big Mama's goal was to retire with no house payment.

Big Mama reached her goal. She retired at sixty-five and died at eighty-two, giving her seventeen years without worrying about a mortgage.

However, times have changed since my grandmother bought her home. In her day, couples bought a home, stayed put for years, and only moved when it was time to retire.

Now couples change houses almost as often as they trade in

cars. People are moving on average every five to seven years and asking if they will always have a house note. The conventional wisdom to pay off a mortgage as soon as you can is no longer conventional. Financial experts now tell folks to get the largest mortgage they can and never worry about paying it off. Naturally, people are confused as to what they should do.

Here's a letter that is typical of the pay-it-off-or-not dilemma: "My wife and I have a running argument, er, discussion, about paying off the mortgage before we retire. She wants to pay it off, thereby 'freeing up' $1,108 a month. I say we're better off not giving the bank a bundle of cash and using the money for other purposes, including investments. She doesn't like debt but I think we can live with it in old age."

Here's another from a confused homeowner: "We have nineteen years remaining on a thirty-year mortgage. The remaining mortgage amount is $58,000, on which we are currently paying an interest rate of 7.5 percent (egad!). This costs us about $1,300 per month. We have the cash to pay off the mortgage (which would still leave us with $150,000 in cash and $600,000 in investments). We have no other debt. Why should we pay 7.5 percent on the mortgage when I can't make that on our money under any current investment scheme? If we should need a large sum of money in the future, then we could take out a home equity loan. Still, something feels strange about parting with all that cash, even though it would save us thousands over the long haul. What are we missing?"

To answer this reader, I consulted two financial planners. First I asked Dee Lee, a certified financial planner and author of *The Complete Idiot's Guide to Retiring Early.*

"I am a big fan of paying off the mortgage on homes," Lee said. If the couple has $358,000 sitting in a money market account paying a puny 2 percent interest—if they're lucky—it would be better for them to pay off the mortgage, she continued. It's a better return on their money, given current stock market conditions. And she advised the couple not to worry about what they would be losing by way of a tax deduction: "Better to have never paid $100,000 in interest than to have paid it and gotten a tax deduction for it."

James R. Cotto, a financial planner based in Mount Kisco, New York, had different advice for the cash-flush couple. He pointed out that the couple's net worth, including the value of their house, is about $1.1 million. If they paid off their mortgage, about 34 percent of their net worth would be tied up in their home. With interest rates near forty-year lows, it makes sense to refinance, Cotto explained. If the couple refinanced and got a fifteen-year mortgage at 5.5 percent, their monthly payment wouldn't go down much—only about $10 a month—but they would save about $65,000 in interest.

Cotto said the couple should consider keeping their cash to invest. Historically stocks have averaged an annual return of about 11 percent since 1926. In addition, real estate should make up no more than approximately 25 percent of an individual's investment portfolio.

So here we are, right back where we started.

If you can, ignore conventional wisdom and think about what's best for you at your particular stage of life. Here are some simple guidelines for different situations:

• **You're a newlywed with no children:** At this stage in your life, concentrate on building up an emergency fund. Studies show you won't be in your house for more than five to seven years, so don't worry about making extra principal payments.

• **You have decades before you have to retire:** With time on your hands, consider boosting your retirement savings rather than paying down your mortgage. Home values have been appreciating steadily, so it's possible that when you sell you'll get a handsome return, making it unnecessary to pile your money into extra mortgage payments.

• **You have small children and want to send them to college:** Right now your priority should be to take any extra money and put it in a 529 plan or mutual fund for your children's college education. You could make extra principal payments, but to tap into that money you may have to incur debt (a home equity loan). Invest the money instead and you won't have to do that.

• **You're nearing retirement:** On average, housing represents between 30 and 40 percent of a household's budget. If you can eliminate your housing expense in retirement, you could have a lot of financial peace and perhaps do that traveling you always wanted to do. So as you get closer to calling it quits, try to pay off your mortgage. You could either aggressively make extra payments on the principal or sell one home and buy a small house outright with the cash you get from your longtime residence.

When it comes to paying off a mortgage, think about your current and future financial needs. But most important, do what lets you sleep at night. If you can't stand having a mortgage, then pay it off.

# 27

---

# HOW MUCH IS
# ENOUGH?

> "You aren't wealthy until you have something money can't buy."
>
> **Garth Brooks**

"How many of you are rich?" my pastor, John K. Jenkins, Sr., asked the congregation one Sunday morning.

You could count on two hands the number of people—out of hundreds sitting in the sanctuary—who raised their hands.

I didn't.

Rich? Me? Hardly.

"Well, you're rich whether you know it or not," Jenkins said. "When you got up this morning, all of you could turn on a faucet and get a drink of water. You didn't have to go down to a river. You walked into a closet with an abundance of clothes. Some of you left the house and could decide which car to take to church. Our animals live in better conditions than some people in the world."

Why didn't I raise my hand?

My pastor knew. I was defining *rich* as having a boatload of money.

After listening to my pastor preach, however, I had to admit that I am rich. I found my Prince Charming. I have three wonderful children. I have a house, cars, and savings. All my basic needs are being met.

And yet, like so many of my fellow congregants, I couldn't bring myself to raise my hand when my pastor asked that simple question.

In fact, the percentage of women and men who feel they have attained the good life remains small, according to a survey released recently by RoperASW. Since 1975, Roper has been tracking how consumers define "the good life." Only 9 percent of those surveyed (more than two thousand adults) felt they had achieved the good life. This despite the fact that a majority of the respondents had the things they said constituted the good life—a house, good health, a car, and children.

"It never ends," Jenkins said during his sermon. "We have a culture of 'got to have, got to drive.'" Nonetheless, even with our need to get more, an overwhelming number of the people in the RoperASW survey said the good life means having good health (87 percent), free time (66 percent), and spiritual well-being (64 percent).

On the other hand, people placed owning a car ahead of having children and a well-paid, interesting job that contributes to the welfare of society. They ranked having a yard or lawn higher than a college education for their children and themselves.

Fifty-two percent of the respondents said a second car is essential to the good life. Forty-eight percent said a vacation home would be necessary.

"I certainly think this and other data illustrate we are definitely a materialistic society," said Ed Keller, Roper's chief executive.

This is good news for marketers, Keller continued. If people can't buy the complete American dream, they can get a piece of it. He called this "affordable approximation"—when companies sell people goods or services that give them a taste of the good life but at a more affordable price.

For example, look at the growth of day spas. Many people can't afford a week at a luxury spa. But they can afford an hour or two of pampering. Many people can't afford a vacation home. So they buy a week of vacation instead. U.S. time-share sales continue to rise, according to a report by Ragatz Associates, a provider of research services to the leisure-travel industry. Approximately 1,600 U.S. time-share resorts serve an estimated three million households.

Keller said he also sees a trend in the auto industry in which luxury-car manufacturers are producing lower-end models of "must-have" cars. And it doesn't seem to bother some consumers that it might take seven years to pay off that "low-end" $30,000 or $40,000 Mercedes.

So if more people are achieving the American dream—albeit only a slice of it—why do so few believe they're living the good life?

"The more we get, the more we want," Keller said. "The bar is always going up for people. If you ask people how much money they need to achieve the American dream, almost always they say two or three times what they make. People are always looking toward the future and toward bettering themselves."

Keller has a point. There's nothing wrong with wanting more.

The problem is, if we keep moving the bar up, when do we ever become content with what we have?

I'll leave you with another question from my pastor: "When will you learn that the pursuit of stuff will not give you internally what will satisfy you?"

Do you have to be rich to be happy?

A lot of people would quickly answer no because, well, that's what you're supposed to say.

The truth is that many people—if they're really honest—believe that if they just had more money, they would be happier.

But does a bigger bank account guarantee your happiness?

As Mother Teresa once said: "Even the rich are hungry for love, for being cared for, for being wanted, for having someone to call their own."

Or as former Federal Reserve chairman Paul A. Volcker said: "What's the subject of life—to get rich? All those fellows out there getting rich could be dancing around the real subject of life."

Living a rich life is largely a state of mind—it's not just about what's on your bank statement. You can stop fighting about money with your man right now if you take that message to heart.

# 28

---

# IT'S NOT ABOUT YOU

For many people in relationships and marriages, the fights about money are rooted in selfishness or a desire to have all things financial split fifty-fifty.

For example, take a look at this statement from a woman who joined me online. She wrote: "My husband and I are newlyweds. We have opened a joint checking account where we each deposit an agreed amount. This account is meant to be used only for shared expenses. I get offended when my husband questions the transactions in this joint account. When I go grocery shopping, I use our joint card. There are times when I accidentally withdraw money from this account to buy things just for me. But I immediately correct the problem. You can even say I go out of my way to make sure that this account is balanced with our equal contributions and the expenditures that only apply to our shared expenses. But every time my husband looks at the account and inquires about each transaction it drives me mad! In the way of background, before we got married we were each extremely independent with our money."

And therein lies their problem and the source of this couple's bickering—they are still extremely independent when they should be depending on each other. Too many couples go into a marriage and refuse to let go of their single thinking. *It's my money. It's my debt. My house. My assets.*

No wonder you're fighting. You are nickel-and-diming yourselves right into the path of a divorce in an effort to make sure you each pay your "fair share." If that's the case, shouldn't you pay less toward your share of the water bill if you take fewer showers? If you only eat one bowl of ice cream from a gallon tub and your husband eats the rest, shouldn't you be entitled to cash back?

You may think I'm being ridiculous, but in principle that's what's happening in modern-day marriages.

If you accept the ground rules for marriage, then you should play by the most important of them—that a marriage means it's not about you anymore. You are a team, with no need to break down and allocate every expense.

Maybe it's not selfishness. Maybe it's fear that is causing the fights—either that your man will take advantage of you or that you'll realize too late that you married a financial fool. Take this letter from a reader: "I am a thirty-one-year-old single woman with no kids. My net worth is more than $300,000, with more than $150,000 in 401(k), Roth IRA, CDs, and index fund, and around $200,000 in home equity. I would like to know how I can protect my assets in case I get married in the future."

Is she going into battle?

If you follow my three Cs for a relationship—communicate, compromise, and set common goals—you won't have to give up your financial freedom or devise an elaborate plan to protect your assets.

Look, I was the classic independent *all-men-are-dogs, I-have-to-*

*have-a-home-wrecking-hussy-account* woman. Then I met and married a man who helped me see the financial light.

The answer isn't to separate. It's to communicate!

You also have to learn to compromise. The apostle Paul says in 2 Corinthians 6:14: "Do not be unequally yoked." That scripture, of course, is about making sure you have a common faith, but the principle or philosophy also works well when it comes to a couple's finances. At the very least, if you are unequally yoked—you're not the same money type—have a jointly agreed-upon plan for how the two of you will deal with your differences.

Finally, establish some common goals. When you're single, you should be independent where your finances are concerned. Once you fall in love and start planning to be married, however, get used to the idea of becoming a part of something bigger than yourself. It's not just about *you* anymore. You should be working to be good stewards over the life riches and wealth that you both can accumulate. You can't do that if you're fighting over which share of the household bills belongs to whom.

One of the beautiful things about being in a marriage is that the whole is greater than the sum of the parts. One plus one can equal more than two!

Even with the divorce rate as high as it is, you and your Prince Charming can get past your financial difficulties if you just stop the selfish behavior and replace your fear with faith. And that faith can only come if you take many of the steps I've outlined in this book. I certainly have faith that you and your man can spend well and live rich.

# PART 4: HOW YOU AND PRINCE CHARMING CAN SPEND WELL AND LIVE RICH

### *What's the Bottom Line?*

Here's what you should have learned from part 4:

✓ If a divorce is imminent—separate your finances completely! Close all joint credit cards right away. If you can, remove your name from all joint loan obligations.

✓ If you want to build a sound financial house, you should start by saving up enough money to cover three to six months of living expenses.

✓ If you're not interested in getting into heavy-duty individual stock investing, the best way to save for your retirement is by buying a mutual fund, either on your own or through your employer-sponsored retirement plan.

✓ Taxes are one of the most significant costs of investing in mutual funds. You need to pay attention to taxes. Buying and selling funds generate capital gains.

✓ Make bonds an important part of your investment portfolio. Bonds may not give you as fast or as high a return as some hotshot stocks, but slow and steady can keep you in the race without giving you a heart attack.

✓ For most people, term life insurance is best. It allows you to buy the most amount of insurance for the least amount of money.

✓ If you're not sure what to do with your money, it may be time to hire a financial planner. Just like you pay to have a bad tooth pulled, pay for a professional to help you avoid bad investing.

✓ We all need to stop and ask ourselves: *How much is enough?* Maybe you're fighting with your spouse because you want too much?

✓ When you get married, it's no longer just about you.

✓ Once you get married, work together to be good stewards of your money.

✓ Follow the three Cs and you and your man can spend well and live rich.

# Acknowledgments

I grew up in a house with a lot of drama. I wrote this book in the hopes that I could help other women avoid at least the financial drama I experienced growing up. But my journey to understanding what it takes to successfully mix money and love is due largely to one person. In fact, this book and the sound financial information I pray it contains wouldn't have been possible without the love of a good, strong man.

I thank God every day (or I should) for leading me to my husband, Kevin. I submit fully to his authority as head of our household. And I can say that without feeling subjugated because my husband leads with kindness, wisdom, and a love for the Lord. He's a wonderful father and friend. My husband showed me how to merge our lives and our money. He taught me to release the fear I had that he would run off with some home-wrecking hussy. I trust him completely with my life, the lives of our children, and, yes, my money.

My grandmother laid the groundwork for the financial common sense I have, but it has been my husband who took that basic training and helped me to improve upon it. Honey, thank you for your advice, patience, and support.

Pastor John K. Jenkins, Sr., your messages about love and money proved to be an inspiration in writing this book. I knew the Lord before you became my pastor, but now I strive to have a deeper relationship with Him. I also value the leadership and love that I get from First Lady Trina Jenkins. Together the two of you are a wonderful example of how a marriage should be and how spouses should treat each other. I'm also gratful that I found a spiritual home at First Baptist Church of Glenarden.

There are some friends and professionals in my life that have been tremendously helpful. Barbara Holt: your professionalism and style have rubbed off on me (I hope). Cory Morgan of Nu-You Wellness & Fitness: despite my constant complaining, thanks for making me work out so hard and teaching me the importance of being physically fit. And Yvonne Bass, my financial advisor at Morgan Stanley: your advice on personal and financial matters has been invaluable.

Again I found myself leaning on a dear friend, Wiley Hall, to help with this book. Wiley, your skills as an editor and writer made this book so much better. I hope you know how much I appreciate your friendship and advice, so often dispensed during long interstate car rides.

To my dear, sweet, awesome, irreplaceable assistant, Lorraine Denis-Cooper, thank you for always having my back and keeping me on schedule and on point. I would be a total wreck without your help. I thank God for finding an assistant who can catch my mistakes, make the calls I can't remember to make, and pray with me even when I'm too weary to lift my head to the sky.

I can't imagine having a better agent. I truly have wonderful representation from Richard Abate of International Creative Management. But the fact is he's not just my agent; he's also a friend. Also much thanks to Maarten Kooij, who has been instrumental in negotiating my entrée into television.

To my editor at Random House, Caroline Sutton: thank you for your patience and suggestions on the book. Christina Duffy, you were such a pleasure to work with. You were always so kind and diplomatic when I e-mailed to say I was going to miss yet another deadline. I appreciated that.

I also couldn't do what I do without the complete support and encouragement of my *Washington Post* family, and especially my editors, Jill Dutt and Nancy McKeon. That goes double for the wonderful team at the Washington Post Writers Group, particularly Jim Hill, Richard Aldacushion, Karen Greene, and Alan Shearer. A special thanks to the team at the Writers Group who work so hard to sell my syndicated column, "The Color of Money," to newspapers around the country and the world. Thanks so much Karisue Wyson, Jennifer Ferrell, Maria Gatti, and Mary Fleming Svensson.

To Russ Walker and the folks at Washingtonpost.com: thanks for helping me create an awesome online presence. Eleanor Hong, I haven't forgotten the many chats you produced.

To Gwendolyn S. King, Jennifer King, and Kelli Bland of Podium Prose: I can't tell you how much it helps to have such a wonderful speaker's bureau representing me.

I also want to thank the many media organizations for whom I work as a contributor. I've worked with Howard University's radio station, WHUR, since I first became a columnist. I can't thank the producers and hosts enough for their support of me and my column. And thanks to the folks at Reach Media, Tom Joyner, Katrina Witherspoon and www.blackamericaweb.com.

I especially have to recognize Alex Chadwick, Kathryn Fox, Shereen Marisol Meraji, and Alicia Montgomery of National Public Radio and "Day to Day." Thank you all for making our work together such a great experience.

To my TV One family, Lee Gaither, Nikki Webber, Johnathan Rodgers, Sitarah Pendleton, and the rest of the wonderful staff: thanks for taking a chance on me and helping to bring my vision to television. And I'll never forget you, Matt Morchower, David Kaufman, and Allyson Brunetti of Varsity Entertainment. You were a wonderful production team.

Finally, but certainly not last in line, I want to acknowledge the support and love of my friends and family, especially my children, Olivia, Kevin, and Jillian. I can't name you all (because if I forget somebody, I won't hear the end of it), but please know I appreciate your being there always. Bless you for the high fives, pats on the back, and for continuing to celebrate my successes and to console me when I'm tired and down. I know I don't call you enough or thank you enough, but know this—I love and value each of you.

# Appendix

## *Resources and Helpful Links*

The following are resources you will find helpful in dealing with your money and your man. Many of the websites listed below follow recommendations listed in the book.

**BUDGETING**

www.budgetingonline.com    Provides consumers with a guide to budgeting.

www.crown.org    A Christian-based website that provides consumers with budget information, including how to get out of debt.

www.MoneyAdvise.com    This website provides budgeting tips and tools.

## BUYING A CAR

www.aaa.com    Offers consumers a plethora of information on researching a vehicle, financing, and car insurance.

www.autosafety.org    Provides consumers with auto safety, fuel economy, and auto defect information. The site also lists lemon laws by state to help lemon owners across the country fight back.

www.carfax.com    Generates a detailed vehicle history report on used cars or light trucks through the use of the unique seventeen-character vehicle identification number (VIN) found on vehicle dashboards and title documents. This service can help reduce the possibility of buying a car that has been in a major accident. Be sure to check with an interested car dealer, because many now offer a free Carfax report.

www.cars.com    This site offers information on new and used cars through partnership with 175 leading newspapers and television stations, and their websites.

www.consumersreport.com    This is an unbiased website that provides independent reviews and information about numerous consumer products, including cars.

www.edmunds.com    A site that helps consumers get a fair deal by providing true market value pricing, unbiased car reviews, ratings, and expert advice.

www.fueleconomy.gov    A great consumer information source for gas mileage, safety, and fuel economy for cars and trucks.

www.lemonaidcars.com    This site provides consumers with information about vehicle defects and abusive auto industry practices. The information is garnered from owner complaints, lawsuits, and judgments, as well as from manufacturer service bulletins and reader warnings.

## BUYING A HOME

www.bankrate.com    Provides consumers with free rate information that includes mortgages, credit cards, new and used automobile loans, money market accounts, and online banking fees, to name a few. It helps consumers make informed financial decisions by publishing original and objective personal finance stories.

www.fanniemae.com    This website provides information to help families achieve the dream of homeownership.

www.freddiemac.com    This website also provides homeownership information.

www.hud.gov    Among other things, this government agency focuses on helping to increase homeownership, supports community development, and advocates increasing access to affordable housing free from discrimination for consumers.

www.nlihc.org    This company is solely dedicated to ending America's affordable housing crisis. Consequently, its advocacy focus is on individuals with the most serious housing problems: those of the lowest-income households.

COLLEGE HELP

www.collegesavings.org   This website provides information in-tended to make higher education more attainable by serving as a clearinghouse for information among existing college savings programs, monitoring federal activities, and promoting legisla-tion that affects state programs.

www.fafsa.ed.gov   This free application for federal student aid (FAFSA) gives students access to the largest source of college finan-cial assistance through grants, work-study programs, and loans.

www.fast.web.com   This is a leading website on local and na-tional scholarships.

www.finaid.org   Provides free consumer access to a comprehen-sive and objective collection of information about financial aid for students searching for ways to finance their education.

www.savingforcollege.com   This site offers independent and objective information about the 529 plan and other ways to save and pay for college. Its goal is to help individuals and profes-sional advisers better understand how to meet the challenge of paying higher education costs.

www.savingsbond.gov   Consumers can buy and redeem securi-ties directly from the U.S. Department of the Treasury in paper-less electronic form.

www.studentaid.ed.gov   The largest source of student finan-cial aid in America, providing nearly 70 percent of all such aid.

Its financial information is designed to assist in college planning while also providing access to information about the products and services needed throughout the financial aid process.

## CREDIT BUREAUS

www.equifax.com    Provides general information for consumers regarding credit, credit scores, and credit reports.

www.experian.com    Provides general information for consumers regarding credit, credit scores, and credit reports as well as preventing identity fraud.

www.transunion.com    Provides general information for consumers regarding credit, credit scores, credit reports, and preventing identity fraud.

## DEBT HELP

www.debtadvice.org    Provides consumers with information on using credit wisely; if necessary, locates certified credit counselors for additional assistance.

www.debtorsanonymous.org    This site provides an arena for men and women to share their financial experiences. Much like Alcoholics Anonymous, participants help one another recover from a shopping compulsion. The only membership requirement is a desire to stop incurring unsecured debt.

## DIVORCE

www.divorce-and-money.com/divorce-donts.shtml   On this site, you will find the top financial mistakes to avoid in a divorce.

www.equalityinmarriage.org   This site provides educational information on the importance of equality in marriage and divorce.

www.wiser.heinz.org   This site is devoted to providing women with the crucial skills and information they need to improve their economic circumstances and plan for a financially sound retirement.

## FINANCIAL PLANNING

www.fpanet.org   This is a membership organization for the financial planners who help consumers make wise financial decisions to achieve their life goals and dreams. On this site you can find certified financial planners.

www.garrettplanningnetwork.com   This site offers a nationwide network of fee-only professional financial advisers who are dedicated to providing competent, objective financial advice to people from all walks of life on an hourly, as-needed basis.

www.investoreducation.com   A great source for investing education.

www.napfa.org   On this site, you can find fee-only financial planners.

**GOVERNMENT HELP**

www.consumer.gov    This site is an online one-stop link to a broad range of federal information resources and is designed to help consumers locate information by category and subcategory.

www.fdic.gov    The Federal Deposit Insurance Corporation insures deposits in banks and thrift institutions.

www.ftc.gov    The Federal Trade Commission provides consumer protection information.

www.house.gov    Here you will find information about your local House representative and other representatives as well as committee hearings, bills, and laws.

www.irs.gov    Believe it or not, this site is very helpful and easy to navigate. It takes you through complex tax issues.

www.occ.treas.gov    The Office of the Comptroller of the Currency serves as regulator and supervisor of all national banks. It issues rules and legal interpretations as well as supervising domestic and international bank activities and also performs corporate analyses.

www.sec.gov    The Securities and Exchange Commission provides regulatory oversight of companies and individuals selling stock.

www.senate.gov    This site gives consumers access to committee hearings, bills, and laws as well as to their senators.

www.studentaid.ed.gov  The largest source of student aid in America, providing nearly 70 percent of all student financial aid. Its financial information is designed to assist in college planning, while also providing access to information about the products and services needed throughout the financial aid process.

### IDENTITY FRAUD

www.anti-phishing.org  This website is run by the Anti-Phishing Working Group, an industry association focused on eliminating the identity theft and fraud that result from the growing problem of "phishing" and "e-mail spoofing." Phishing is what con artists do when they go "fishing" for people's personal financial information by pretending to be representatives of legitimate companies and government agenies. E-mail spoofing is forging an e-mail header to make it appear as if it came from somewhere or someone other than the actual source.

### INSURANCE

www.acli.com.  The American Council of Life Insurers offers a brochure called *How to Buy Life Insurance* that is very useful.

www.iii.org  The Insurance Information Institute is another good site with basic insurance information.

www.insure.com  This is an excellent site that provides a great deal of information about all types of insurance (home, car, life, et cetera).

www.life-line.org. Try the life-insurance-needs calculator created by the Life and Health Insurance Foundation for Education.

## INVESTING

www.better-investing.org This company is an independent, non-profit, member-driven organization committed to teaching individuals how to become successful, strategic long-term investors.

www.dallasfed.org On this site, you will find a useful guide to building wealth produced by the Federal Reserve Bank of Dallas.

www.ici.org/quiz/getthefactsquiz.html On this site, you can test your knowledge of mutual funds with questions prepared by the Investment Company Institute.

www.investoreducation.org This website is run by the Alliance for Investor Education. It provides a wide range of basic investor information.

www.nasaa.org This website's main purpose is to protect consumers who purchase securities or investment advice.

www.sec.gov/investor/pubs/inws.htm. This link provides tips on how to select a broker and invest wisely.

www.sharebuilder.com Share Builder is an online brokerage company that has set up a low-cost and easy system for people to invest.

## LOANS

www.lifeadvice.com   This site provides an abundance of information to consumers regarding insurance, banking, investment and planning services, and more.

www.loanconsolidation.ed.gov   Provides loan-consolidation information to borrowers, schools, and loan holders, and answers many consumer-related questions regarding loan consolidation on its FAQ page.

## RETIREMENT CALCULATORS

www.bankrate.com/brm/calculators/retirement.asp.   If you are unsure of how much you will need in order to retire, try this calculator. It's one of the better ones.

www.choosetosave.org   Offers a ballpark estimate retirement planning worksheet.

www.finance.cch.com   Here you will find two dozen calculators to help with your retirement planning.

www.homefair.com   This site allows you to see how far your income will go in various cities.

www3.troweprice.com/ric/RIC   The T. Rowe Price calculator helps you determine if your retirement savings and investments will last. It incorporates a simulator to show you how certain factors can affect your plans for a steady income.

www.vanguard.com/VGApp/hnw/RetirementSavings   The
Vanguard calculator can help you come up with some retirement
saving goals. You will also get tips on how to reach those goals.

## SAVING

www.choosetosave.org   A resourceful site that provides financial
tools to help consumers of all ages plan every aspect of their financial security while promoting the idea that saving today is essential to securing a financial future.

www.icfe.info   This website provides information that helps
people of all ages improve their spending, increase their savings,
and use credit more wisely.

www.saveforyourfuture.org   Provides saving tools and other
program information to inform consumers about saving and
planning for retirement as well as other life stages.

## SENIORS

www.aarp.org/money   AARP is a nonprofit, nonpartisan membership organization for people fifty and older that provides information on and resources for financial planning and
retirement, Social Security, credit and debt, mortgages, and
other sources for the maintenance of a healthy financial life.

www.caremanager.org   A nonprofit association of professional
practitioners dedicated to humane and dignified social, psycho-

logical, and health care for the elderly and their families through counseling, treatment, and services.

www.eldercare.gov   A nationwide service that connects older Americans and their caregivers with information on senior services. It is designed to identify trustworthy local support resources to help older adults, their families, and their caregivers find their way through the maze of services for seniors while also helping older people live independently and safely in their homes and communities for as long as possible.

www.reversemortgage.org   Provides information to consumers interested in learning more about reverse mortgages. (A reverse mortgage is available only to homeowners age sixty-two or older and allows seniors to convert equity in their home into tax-free cash without selling or giving up title.)

## SOCIAL SECURITY STATEMENT

www.socialsecurity.gov/mystatement   Find out how much you can expect to get in Social Security benefits.

# Index

gift registries, 94–95

*see also* engagements

Wendt, Lorna Jorgenson, 57

whole life insurance, 228–29

Williams, Catherine, 117

wills

and minor children, 179, 182–84

money milestones, 19, 20, 21

reasons for having, 7

what to include, 183–84

women

African-American, 5

age 20–29 milestones, 18–19

age 30–39 milestones, 20–21

age 40–49 milestones, 21

age 50 and older, 21–22

caregiver responsibilities, 4

financial planning steps, 6–9

life expectancy, 4

single, 6–9, 230–31

and Social Security, 4

statistics, 4–5

as stay-at-home mothers, 165–70

years in workforce, 4

**Z**

Zemsky, Robert, 195

## ABOUT THE AUTHOR

MICHELLE SINGLETARY's *Washington Post* column, "The Color of Money," is now syndicated in more than 130 newspapers across the country. She is the host of *Singletary Says* on the cable network TV One, as well as a regular contributor to NPR's *Day to Day*, and has appeared on MSNBC, CNBC, *Nightline*, *The Oprah Winfrey Show*, *The View*, and *The Diane Rehm Show*. Singletary is a graduate of the University of Maryland and has a master's degree in business from Johns Hopkins University. For more than fifteen years, she has covered business and personal finance, first for the Baltimore *Evening Sun* and then for *The Washington Post*. She lives in Maryland with her husband and three children. Visit her website at www.michellesingletary.com.

## ABOUT THE TYPE

This book was set in Garamond, a typeface originally designed by the Parisian type cutter Claude Garamond (1480–1561). This version of Garamond was modeled on a 1592 specimen sheet from the Egenolff-Berner foundry, which was produced from types assumed to have been brought to Frankfurt by the punch cutter Jacques Sabon (d. 1580).

Claude Garamond's distinguished romans and italics first appeared in *Opera Ciceronis* in 1543–44. The Garamond types are clear, open, and elegant.